HOW TO BUILD THE TEAM YOU WANT

(And Lead Them To Victory!)

Marco Kelly

Marco Kelly

Marco Kelly

© Copyright 2019 - All rights reserved.

The content contained within this book may not be reproduced, duplicated or transmitted without direct written permission from the author or the publisher.

Under no circumstances will any blame or legal responsibility be held against the publisher, or author, for any damages, reparation, or monetary loss due to the information contained within this book. Either directly or indirectly.

Legal Notice:

This book is copyright protected. This book is only for personal use. You cannot amend, distribute, sell, use, quote or paraphrase any part, or the content within this book, without the consent of the author or publisher.

Disclaimer Notice:

Please note the information contained within this document is for educational and entertainment purposes only. All effort has been executed to present accurate, up to date, and reliable, complete information. No warranties of any kind are declared or implied. Readers acknowledge that the author is not engaging in the rendering of legal, financial, medical or professional advice. The content within this book has been derived from various sources. Please consult a licensed professional before attempting any techniques outlined in this book.

By reading this document, the reader agrees that under no circumstances is the author responsible for any losses, direct or indirect, which are incurred as a result of the use of information contained within this document, including, but not limited to, — errors, omissions, or inaccuracies.

Contents

Introduction
The Recruitment Process
   Every Job Is Yours
   The Interview Process
   Selection and Hiring
   The Orientation
Training and Coaching
   The Process of Transition
   The Puzzle Pieces
   Repeat, Repeat And Have Them Repeat Back
   Do Not Overwhelm & Do Not Underwhelm
   Train the Trainer & Quiz
   Evaluations
   The Discipline Process
Leadership
   The Leadership Profile
   Genuine Care
   Decisive
   Balanced
   Empowering
   Flexible
   Evolving
   Honesty and Your Word
   Inspire
The Leadership Tool Box
   Dragnet Beginning
   Parental Approach
   Directive Approach
   Confrontational Approach
   Collaborative Approach

Educational Approach
Motivational Approach
Communicative Approach
Evaluative Approach
Accountability Approach
Mirror Approach
Interrogative Approach
Mediator Approach
Catalyst Approach
Incentive Approach

The Finish Line

INTRODUCTION

If you have ever said: "I need good people!" your words have been echoed by nearly every business owner, operator and manager that I have ever met, and most likely everyone that you have met as well. I recently saw the following comment on FaceBook: "I need cooks." It was posted by a friend who owns a restaurant in Northern Ontario and is, as most restaurant owners and operators are, in dire need of good cooks.

During many conversations with business operators, and from my own experiences, it is very evident that many staffing issues are plaguing the workplace. I have heard some try to attribute these issues to Generation Y, but while there are some definite challenges with this new group of young people coming into the workforce, from my experience, there are challenges that exist on all levels. The old saying: 'Good people are hard to find' is just that; an old saying. Staffing issues are not a new thing because of Generation Y; they have always existed. Moreover, while Generation Y requires some major paradigm shifts for Managers, I believe staffing issues continue to exist because of a perpetuation of the ineffective practices of hiring, training, and leading.

The reason this book is written is to answer the question of how to change the cycle and build the team you want in your organization, and how then to lead them to success. I hope to accomplish just that.

One of the first things to understand is the importance of team strength. We all know the old saying that the chain is only as strong as the weakest link and nothing could be more accurate. If you have a team where one of your individuals is consciously or unconsciously sabotaging the efforts and results of the other members, it certainly affects the overall strength of the team. That being said, the value of a team even with a weak link is still generally more valuable than a link all by itself. Think of a brick. What are the uses of a brick all by itself? Some possibilities include a paperweight, a doorstop or a small step. Now think of that brick with a thousand other bricks, what are the potential uses of that brick now? So do not try to do everything yourself. Rather than exerting extra effort trying to do all the tasks, use the energy to diligently train, develop and lead your team to ensure those tasks are completed to the highest of standards.

However, let's go back to the bricks for a second. Understanding that the strength of a wall is impacted by the quality of the bricks used is essential. If you use rotten or cracked bricks, it is safe to say that your wall will not be solid. However, it is also safe to say that if you use perfect, durable, high-quality bricks, but the mortar you use to put them together is faulty, then the strength of your wall will also be significantly compromised.

One of the best analogies I can use to describe what I mean here is a music group or band. You could take five musicians and put them together. While they have to practice and develop their abilities on their instrument individually, they also have to learn to play in harmony with each other. If four of the five players are good, and the fifth one is not very good, how will it impact the sound of the group as a whole?

The strength of the team as a whole is greater than the sum of the individual strengths of the musicians. You can also have five musicians whom each plays exceptionally well but they do not get along, and this creates a lot of tension and negativity. Can you imagine how will that impact the quality of the music the band plays? The reality is that all of it matters.

As you read through this book, you will learn about the essential steps of ensuring that you are choosing high quality and strong 'bricks for your wall' or 'musicians for your band.' You will also learn some valuable essential tools along the way about how to make sure you are pulling them together. You want to create cohesion, so they work well together with mutual purpose and become a strong and successful team, a team of which you are proud to be the leader.

One of the critical elements in team building is in helping each member of the team understand that the value of the team is greater than the sum of the values of the individuals. The importance of the team is greater than the significance of the individuals on the team. Moreover, the accomplishments that the team can realize as a team are far more significant than all the achievements each of the members of the team can achieve individually.

In addition to team building, like with the musicians, there is also the element of how you inspire, motivate and lead the individuals on the team and how you focus on their individual development and performance.

I once worked for a company where we sold office supplies. My boss at the time was a very charismatic fellow, but he had a couple of significant flaws as a leader; he could be a bit negative and was also a tad ego driven and looked to make every win for the company his own. This approach served to undermine significantly the motivation of the individuals on his team, which in turn affected their performance.

The truth is that I was a mediocre salesperson. I hit my numbers, but I was by far not a trendsetter for the company. After being there for about six months, a few members of the team, I included, went to Vancouver to work with our West Coast teams and I was partnered up with a young, bright, positive manager. We worked together for about a week, and although I learned a lot from him, the most significant impact he had on me was in teaching that building a positive, focused mindset translates directly into success.

I did not quite learn it at the time, but after going through the whole process and doing the post-mortem analysis, I was able to put the various pieces of the puzzle together that allowed me to see the entire picture.

I returned home from that week in BC and had the best sales week I had ever had. I was on a high, I was motivated, I was pumped, and I had no fear. I walked into a prospect account I had been delaying going into for a while and walked out with the biggest order for products I had ever written.

After that first fantastic week back, I started to notice that my energy began to fade. It felt like my battery was dying. I was losing steam fast and not long after I found myself back in the slump.

From analyzing this experience, I learned a few things.

Your success is highly dependent on your mindset. We are what we think about, and if you are thinking of failure as opposed to focusing on the steps that lead to success, your failure is imminent.

Your success is highly dependent on your energy. If you do not have the energy and drive to push hard to do what needs to get done to achieve success, it is not going to happen.

People can inspire you to achieve great things, if you let them, by changing your mindset. Also, you can do the same for others.

If you allow it, people can inject you with energy, or if you let it, people can drain your energy and keep you down. It is up to you where you look for inspiration and motivation. Evaluate what you are getting and determine whether it is helping you achieve your goals, or keeping you from them.

So, with that analysis, I began the journey of learning how to find a way to inject myself with the energy and inspiration necessary to achieve great things. This is a tough job, which is why we mostly look to others to build us up and to inspire us. Although it helps if you are doing something about which you are you are passionate.

When we are inspired we adopt new philosophies, start making some new choices and start to see better results. These results then become the Catalyst to adopt more new beliefs, and we then make further new choices. We evaluate our findings and determine whether they are the results we want. So if the results are moving us towards our goal, we keep pushing forward fueled by our progress. One key point here is the goal, or the "What I want," but we'll get to that later.

When the results are not what we want, we can usually just change tactic and keep pushing, but sometimes it can affect us negatively. When this happens, we might experience a moment of doubt and then drive through it and carry on. Sometimes, however, we may fall into a slump and can stay there until we either talk ourselves out of it or we turn to someone for help. Sometimes we need someone to give us some inspiration to help us get back on the trail to start moving forward again.

I have discovered that there are people in this world who are excellent at bouncing back and pushing through. They succeed at everything they put their minds to and never accept failure. Even when they do fail, they take that failure as learning and use that knowledge and education to help them achieve success. These people are, in my observations, uncommon.

These are the people who generally find themselves at the top of whatever field they are in whether it is sports, entertainment or business. Because these people are rare, it is unwise to expect this behavior from everyone on your team. Moreover, as Gandhi so eloquently put it, "Be the change you wish to see in the world."

Your job as leader of your organization is to help your team buy into new and better philosophies that would propel them forward to better results, inspire them to use those results to build momentum and to continue to do this until your team is achieving a level of success they only dreamed they could achieve.

Looking to others for inspiration is the reason that the Self-Help Book and Motivational Speaking industries exist: to give the inspiration designed to be the catalyst of change that propels you forward to higher heights. It has been said, however, that most people do not read the self-help books they purchase. Most lay on shelves or desks gathering dust while the owner claims to be too busy to open and digest the wisdom they believed they needed when they bought the book. I hope this one does not share that fate.

THE RECRUITMENT PROCESS

A different approach

Having the right people on your team to help you accomplish your goals and objectives is necessary to take your company where you want or need it to go. Maybe you do not have enough people, or perhaps you merely recognize that on your team some of the people you ¬¬have are not the right people. Either way, your first step may not be what you think.

You might think your first step is to put an ad in the paper or on a job search website letting the general public know that you are in search of new team members. The chances are that is the first step you have always taken in the past, and if so, this has led you to where you are now. As the old saying goes, if you always do what you always did, you will always get what you always got.

If you want something different, you gotta do something different.

This starts by taking a different approach to the process.

The first thing to do is create the Vision for your company and determine the type of culture you would like to develop and foster within your organization.

Put much thought into this: Where you want to be, how to get there and whom you need to help you get there. The Vision for your company, organization, department or Team is the key that ties everything else together. Imagine working on a puzzle. You have two thousand puzzle pieces in front of you. Now, without the picture on the box as a reference point, how successful would you be in putting that puzzle together? My guess is not very. Alternatively, it would take you a very long time to do it, spending many unnecessary and frustrating hours of trial and error. Also, how can you teach someone else to put the puzzle together if you do not have the picture on the box? Could you give a hundred pieces to twenty different people, and ask them to work with each other to put the puzzle together without the picture on the box? They might get it done eventually, but it would undoubtedly take much time, cause a lot of arguments and frustration and, in the end, would not generate a good return on investment.

Your Vision is essentially the picture on the box. You need it so you know how the pieces should fit together, and your team needs it, so they know what they need to do and how to work together to complete the puzzle. No Vision, no success.

Committing to the Vision is the second step. You can create the most amazing Vision, but if you are not committed to it, it will not matter. I have narrowed the elements of life to the six key areas: Accomplishments, Career, Finance, Fitness & Health, Relationships, and Spirituality. To achieve success in any of these areas, you would need to have a Vision for that area and commit to it. The reality is that you can only achieve a level of success in any area of your life equal to the level of your commitment to the Vision you have for that area in your life. If you have no Vision, you will not achieve success. If you have a Vision, but you are not committed to it, you will not achieve success. However, if you have a Vision and you are one hundred percent committed to it, you will achieve success. Why? Because your commitment will force you to consistently evaluate every choice you make to determine whether it is moving you towards your goal, or keeping you from it. My favorite example is Fitness. With Fitness, you are very aware of whether you are moving towards your goal, or if your choices, actions, and behavior are preventing you from achieving it. If you have a Vision for your fitness and you are one hundred percent committed to it, it will dramatically affect the choices you are making every day regarding what and how you are eating, making sure you are drinking your water, staying active, working out, and so on. You cannot expect to hang out on the couch, eating junk food and drinking pop and expect to achieve any success with your fitness goals, right?

Another excellent example of this is Finances. If your goal is to be debt free, you know you cannot keep putting purchases on your credit cards. You know you cannot keep buying things you do not need and expect that you are going to be successful with your finances. Your commitment to your goal does not allow you to make choices that impede your ability to achieve it. That is the importance of having a Vision, and the importance of committing to it.

Your actions and choices will always reflect your commitment. Talk is cheap, but actions are the proof. Saying you are committed is one thing, but it doesn't matter if you don't follow through by living it.

Part of the process of creating the Vision is determining what the various levels of needs are for your company, group, organization or department, but also what is the critical difference you would like to make. What separates your company from every other company like it out there? What is your Point of Difference?

One of the ways of achieving a deep understanding of what is most meaningful to you is to ask yourself fifty times "What do I want to achieve with my company?" and write down your answers. In the initial stage, do not worry too much about the validity of every response, it is a process. You are asking your brain to dig and sometimes it will throw up bones, but you still keep digging until you find the treasure. In the end, you should be able to condense that list to your top ten, and then the top three and then your number one. Usually, the more you dig; the more profound you start to get. The process can be very enlightening and rewarding, but remember to have fun with it.

Your final answer should be very aligned with your core goal in life. Moreover, aligning everything you do to that core goal is crucial to keeping you committed and passionate about your Vision. That passion is what will help to fuel your energy and inspiration and will also help you get the buy-in from the members of your team. Getting behind someone passionate and committed to achieving greatness is often far more successful than trying to get behind someone who is not 'in it to win it.'

People all want to be a part of something great. What does your slice of greatness look like, and how can you get the people on your team to see it?

Keep this all top of mind before and during the processes of building your team, because after you have built your team and things are moving along, helping your team understand this Vision, and the importance of it, gives your team a sense of mutual purpose. Everything they do can be relayed back to the Vision to determine whether their choices and actions are creating movement toward the Vision, or away from it. The Vision becomes the beacon for the team and toward which everyone focuses on moving.

If everyone is pushing forward, in the same direction, with intensity, determination, and purpose, it is hard to believe that you cannot succeed. Imagine a group of people trying to push out a car that is stuck in the mud. If, because the goal and plan were ineffectively communicated, not everyone is pushing in the same direction it can create a neutralization of energies, and the result is very little success. If, however, everyone is pushing in the same direction then the energies are joined, and the result is an excellent success. Now, that analogy is a silly one because in that situation it is easy to see if people are pushing in the wrong direction.

The problem with most organizations is in not being able to see when people are pushing in the wrong direction until after the fact because it is not as visually evident. Even if you ask them what direction they are pushing in, they might tell you what they think is the right answer, even though their actions and choices are not consistent with that direction. It may also be that they have not been able to make the connection between their actions and the outcome. They may be completely unaware that their efforts are working in contradiction with the desired objective. In most cases, however, the cause is usually a lack of commitment to the Vision and the goals of the company, an uncertainty as to what they are, or a combination of the two.

That is why it is so important to keep reinforcing the Vision for yourself and your team and design barometers and systems to allow you to have clear evidence of the direction each member of your team is pushing in. However, we will get to more on that later.

With this in mind, you needn't wait for the new hires. You can begin to implement and communicate the principles and strategies of your Vision to your existing team to start creating this culture. It then becomes easier for whom you hire to step into stride with this current winning culture.

Marco Kelly

Every Job Is Yours

Imagine that every job in the department or company is your job and you know you can't do all the posts at the same time, so the point of hiring is to bring people in to help you do those jobs. It then becomes more evident that the people you bring in should be able to help you, not just fill the position. You do not just want warm bodies on the floor; you want people pushing that car out of the mud, and in the right direction.

When you approach it this way, you begin to see the framework of what you need and how to start.

Having a clear understanding in your mind of the types of people you need in your organization is immensely important. You need people of good character, the kind of attitude that would make them capable of assisting in the building and maintaining of the new culture.

Remember that there are certain things that you cannot teach or develop within people — things like drive, ambition, attention to detail, loyalty, determination, and self-motivation.

If you focus on hiring people who have natural abilities or talents in these areas, your job will become far more enjoyable and rewarding.

If you hire people who are deficient in these categories, then you will always be facing some massive challenges with performance issues.

For the duties they will attend to in the position you are filling, which skills are necessary that they have experience, and which can you invest in training?

How To Build The Team You Want

To get an idea of their team-player experience, you can look at where they have worked or what kind of team sports have they played. If they already have Team experience, that is a good thing, as they will most likely have learned the importance of functioning as a team. You may still have some work to do, but you would have a head start.

Do they need to have worked in this position before, or can you train them from the ground up if they have the right character profile?

If the candidates need to have some training or experience; what level and how much?

Concerning character, determine what some of the crucial elements for the various positions might be. If you need them to deal with customers, being friendly and confident would be good. If they are going to be sweeping the floors of a warehouse, while it would be nice to have those attributes, they are not necessary. You may prefer to have attention to detail and a sense of urgency with the floor sweeper.

For elements of performance, consider the following attributes:

Attention to Detail, Communication, Completes Tasks, Engaged, Focused, Follow Up, Follows Instructions, Follows Procedures, Leadership, Organized, Preparation, Productivity, Punctual, Sense of Urgency, Timely

Moreover, for elements of character, consider these attributes:

Amiable, Coachable, Committed, Courteous, Helpful, Honesty, Listens well, Positive, Respectful, Responsible, Self-Motivated, Self-Control, Supportive, Teamwork, Tolerance/Acceptance

You can review each attribute for the position and classify them as a 'Need,' a 'Want,' a 'Nice to have' and a 'Not Necessary.' In the end, you pull out your needs and headline them, then your wants, and so on.

Now you have a profile of character (which relates to attitude), and experience (which speaks to performance and ability).

This step should be completed for each position in your company or department.

I know in my personal experiences, if I have to choose between experience and character, I would sacrifice experience and choose character every time. I can teach and train someone who has a natural drive to succeed at whatever they do, but I cannot teach an experienced person to have a right attitude, to be passionate or to be driven in the pursuit of excellence. If that is not in their nature, nothing I do will change that.

Once you have these things clear in your mind, you can then place your ad in the paper or website. Have your ad describe the type of person for whom you are looking. Not only to potentially alleviate the number of people replying to it who will be a waste of your time and theirs, but it is also the first step in setting the expectations of what you will be holding them accountable for if they are selected for the position.

Doing this makes it rather difficult for someone to say: "I did not sign up for this" when the duties, standards, and objectives have been laid out in the very ad to which they have replied. From there, the interview and orientation process should be consistent with the Vision you have of what you need to build and maintain the type of culture you know will propel your company to success.

Attracting top talent is tough. So your ad can also be an opportunity to briefly promote your Value Proposition concerning what you have to offer a good candidate. This serves to attract individuals who may not be actively looking but may entertain the idea of switching companies if they believe the opportunity you are offering is better than the one they have.

How To Build The Team You Want

Take a moment before moving on to the next chapter to complete the exercises listed in this chapter.

- Create a Vision for your company or department.
- Identify the culture you need in the organization that serves the Vision.
- Create a character profile for each position for the type of person you need.
- Create a system to evaluate if the team members are all pushing in the same direction.
- Begin implementing your Vision with your existing team to build the culture before the new candidates arrive.

If a part of your new culture is to help your team members achieve some personal goal or milestone, have your existing team members write out their bucket list and hand them into you. Communicate that you will do all you can to help them achieve at least one item on their list. This culture builds on the law of reciprocity where if your team believes that you are willing to break through walls for them, then they will be willing to break through walls for you.

The Interview Process

So, by now, if you have followed the recommendations from chapter one, you will have a full profile of character and experience for each position in your department or organization. Also, if you are to gain the most out of these processes, you will have written them down. A goal that is not written down is merely a wish. The method of writing them out not only solidifies the concepts within your mind, but it also makes it easier to share them with those who may be assisting you in the hiring of new team members.

The questions you ask during the interview process should be designed to help you understand whether or not your potential candidate fills the bill. The process could be compared to going out on a date. You ask questions to see if the person you are out with is a good fit for you.

It would be best that you do not come right out and ask typical or specific questions as that might only result in getting the "what they think you want to hear" answers. Instead, create a dialogue that lets the other person open up about her values, ethics, philosophies, and perception of the world and herself. Then you take all the information and process it down to a summary that you compare to your character profile sheet. You might come across the opportunity where you were interviewing for one position, but find that they have the ideal profile for a different job.

Understand that the types of questions you ask can build your credibility as a leader with your candidate, and can help them think differently about the job and begin to see it more of an opportunity to grow and advance rather than just a paycheck to take care of the basic needs of roof, food, water and so on. In the end, people want to be a part of a winning team.

Asking questions and then asking them to qualify their answers is a great strategy.

Questions like:

What are your personal goals for this position?

What steps do you plan to take to achieve those goals?

Or

What is your service philosophy?

How would you apply that philosophy in the day to day duties?

Or

What does success mean to you?

How do you see yourself being able to contribute to the success of this company?

What you are also trying to do is to lay the foundation for presenting the position you are filling as an integral part of your business, which it is. Regardless of what position you are hiring for, it exists because it is necessary to maintain your business. Treat them as such and put that weight behind them when you are recruiting.

If you say: "Well, I do not care about this position so I'll just grab someone and get them working." You take a significant chance of hiring someone who is not the right fit for your company culture. Furthermore, they will probably learn to adopt your views about the position, and it will negatively impact your business.

You might say: "Well, I do not care about my dishwashers, they just wash dishes, and any fool can do that." Remember that whomever you hire is going to be instrumental in maintaining proper sanitation for your kitchen, food-service tools and in what and with what your customers are going to be eating. If they do not adequately fulfill their duties, your customers may receive dirty cutlery or glassware, or worse get sick from cross-contamination in their food from improperly washed equipment or cookware. There may also be health and safety concerns in the kitchen. While the position does not require a Master's degree in engineering, it does need someone who understands the importance of the role and who has the attention to detail to not send out coffee cups with lipstick on them.

If you do not care about the people who stock your shelves, or load your trucks, or answer your phones, or clean your rooms, or file your papers or greet your customers, chances are they will not care much either, and your customers will feel and see it. There would be a very dramatic difference between your company and a company where those people and positions are considered essential elements in the overall business.

It may also be helpful to remember that the level of importance you put on the positions in your company will generally be more than what the person in the job puts on it. So if you do not put much importance on a position, the person in that position puts even less. So, with that line of thinking, you need to grasp the real significance of every position in your place of business and understand that without that position, everything else falls.

During the interview process, this is your opportunity with the candidate to let them know the level of importance you place on this position, what your expectations are for the successful candidate and ask them if they are capable of rising to that challenge.

The value of those types of questions, and of the candidates stating their willingness and ability to accomplish what you have laid out as the duties and responsibilities associated with the position, is that all you have to do from then on is hold them accountable to what they said and consistently reinforce their commitments to you.

After the interview, the best outcome is that you walk away

knowing you have the right person to select on the team. The second best outcome is that you walk away knowing they are not the right person. The worse thing to happen is to not identify with any degree of certainty whether you have the right person or not because then you will have to wait and see. You are better off, if you are not sure, of asking more questions to help you get a better idea of whether it should be a yes or a no.

Sometimes we fall into the trap of hiring someone who is not what we need but who is better than some you have interviewed and you want to grab them before someone else does. From my personal experience, this usually ends in one of two ways:

Either they quit in a short time, or you wished they did.

Sometimes you hire what you believe to be the closest facsimile to what you are looking for from the options you have available to you. There's nothing wrong with that. Sometimes it is necessary, but it is important to note the two critical factors to consider when hiring someone who does not meet all the criteria you have set:

- The deficiencies are not the non-negotiable elements of either character or experience
- The weaknesses are ones that you can train or develop.

Be careful about getting attached to people and failing to decide to move out your low performers when you receive applications from people who are better than someone you already have. This is known as staff cycling and is regarded as a best practice for making your team better. The process is done by switching out players who are holding the team back from achieving greatness, your low performers, and replacing them with new players who possess better skills, attitudes and experience.

I was once asked by a member of a team I was leading: "If you place such an importance on the team, how can you let players go?" My response was to state that it is because I place so much importance on the team that I can let players go. The team is important, more important than any of the individual players. If any player is hurting the team, I would be remiss in my duties to allow that player to continue to do so, especially when faced with the opportunity of bringing a stronger player into the fold.

As leaders, we cannot allow our personal feelings or compassion for people to cloud our judgment about what is best for the business. I had let people go when it broke my heart to do so because they failed to deliver the performance necessary despite numerous attempts to develop them. The decision always comes back to their Performance, Character and the impact they have on the business.

So, even when you have a full crew and do not require players, still keep your eye out for new players and look to strengthen your team by making a few trades. Remember, the success of your business is dependent almost entirely on the strength of your team, including your Managers. Value each member, look for opportunities to develop them and get them where you need them to be. However, if they demonstrate that they are either incapable or unwilling to get there, it is time to look for the opportunity to make a trade. So, always be interviewing, you never know whom you will find.

Other great questions to ask are:

- Tell me about the types of interaction you had with other workers at your last job?
- Of all the jobs you have had, which did you like the least? Why?
- Tell me of a work-related accomplishment that you are particularly proud of and describe what you did.
- What kind of guidance and support do you expect from your manager?
- In your last job, did you run into any difficult situations? How did you handle them?
- Have you ever been mismanaged? How did it affect you? What did you do about it?

- Why did you leave your last two jobs?
- What do you think could happen to hinder your success?
- What specific kind of work do you most enjoy doing?

The specifics of the answers are not that important, but how they answer can serve to reveal much about who they are and how they think. Also, remember to qualify answers with follow up questions. This helps to let you know if they are telling you what they think you want to hear.

Take a moment before moving on to the next chapter to complete the exercises listed in this chapter.

- Evaluate the importance of each position in your company or department. Consider how your company or department would perform without that position.
- Create a list of questions to ask your candidate. Consider if the questions you propose would be different for the various positions.
- Create a list of the type of answers you are looking for and how they would tie in with the character profile you have prepared for the various positions.
- Practice asking these questions with friends or trusted colleagues and practice asking follow up questions.

Selection and Hiring

So, at this point, you have created your profiles, and you have interviewed a few candidates. You have asked questions to inspire dialogue that would give you a good sense about who they are and whether they are truly capable of helping you, and the team, achieve the goals and objectives you face.

Some people think that they need to nab someone before someone else nabs them, but before we jump the gun and grab someone, there's a little homework to do: The reference check.

Use one of the best tools you have available to you to determine whether you are going down a road of trouble or reward. It should only take about half an hour or so.

The chances of losing them in half an hour are slim, and the half an hour invested could save you hours of headache, maybe weeks of aggravation, and possibly be right back where you are in a few days or weeks.

Before we get into the specifics of the reference checks, allow me to take a moment to caution you on what is considered to be humankind's biggest addiction. No, I'm not talking drugs, or alcohol, or gambling. I am talking about the need to be right.

People, in general, need to be right. This need is such a powerful addiction that if we believe something to be true we can, and will, ignore all the evidence or facts that point to a conclusion that differs from our existing beliefs.

The thing about truth is that we all have our version of it. We can, and will, twist the truth in our minds until it fits with our beliefs. If you believe someone to be a bad person, you will not see the good things they do, and you will only notice the bad and say:

"See? I told you he was bad!"

The point of me writing all this is to caution you that when doing a reference check, try not to have a predetermined idea of whether the candidate is a great pick or not. Just go in completely open-minded and evaluate the responses you get.

Reference checks are challenging with the privacy laws, and everyone seems to be very cautious and careful about giving negative references. A few large corporations have been the victims of a big lawsuit from ex-employees who were given negative references. Those ex-employees then sued those corporations for defamation of character.

The way around that is only to ask questions that would help you ascertain if the previous employer viewed the candidate as a valuable Team Member. Ask the types of questions that are in alignment with the concepts we talked about in the Recruitment Process. You know who you want, you have chatted with them, and now you want some history that lets you see if they can walk the talk.

Questions like:

Would you hire them back?

Did he/she help you in achieving the team's goals?

Would the rest of the team be happy if they came back to work for you?

These questions are closed-ended; direct questions that do not require elaboration on the part of the answerer. They do not need the references to go into a dialogue of the candidate's abilities or performance. From a simple yes or no their answers tell you a lot about the character of the individual from the standpoint of contribution to the company, and that is the essential information.

If the answers to those questions are a consistent "Absolutely!" Then you know you have a winner on your hands. If they are delayed, unclear, muddy or a simple no, then the right thing to do would be to pass.

A key point in reference checks is not to only call the references they give you. No one is going to provide you with the name of someone they know is not going to provide them with a glowing recommendation. If the references are previous Managers, then it would be wise to call them, but also look for companies listed on their resume where a reference has not been given.

Now, do all of the references have to be glowing? Not necessarily. We know that people have off days, or sometimes they were going through a tough time, and it may have impacted their work. What we are looking for is a pattern. If the overall trend is positive, you are ok. If it seems mostly negative, you know what you have to do. The challenge is when it is inconclusive, and you are back to relying on your gut.

The truth is there is no science to this. Just some best practices to alleviate the chance of hiring the wrong person for the company. In the end, you might still have to listen to your gut and take a chance. However, as I have said before, do not be attached to your decisions. If you find you have made a wrong call, fix it immediately. Do not wait. The longer you wait, the tougher it gets. Remember, it is not about individuals. It is about the team.

After this is completed and you have made your selection, you may now contact the successful candidate and set up the next step. Calling everyone else you interviewed to inform them that you have not chosen them is a wise step as well. You might come across them again, and they will have more respect for you if you have called them to let them know you went another way.

The next step is the offer negotiation where you lay out what your compensation package includes as in benefit options, perks, and other elements. From there the candidate reviews your offering and either accepts, rejects or negotiates.

Negotiation is a touchy thing, and the best way to approach is to try to create a win/win and focus on the interests of your candidate without compromising your interests. Find out what he/she wants and compare that to what you are prepared to offer and see where the middle ground is. Depending on the position, this can be a simple matter or a tug-of-war. Do not try to guess what the most essential element for the candidate is and push that. Find out what is most important to the candidate. He may be looking for the benefits to start on the same day he starts the position as opposed to having to wait the traditional three or six months. He may not be as concerned with the salary number. Alternatively, an extra vacation week might be more important. Ask some questions about his or her needs, wants and expectations and then try to tailor a package that suits them. This usually works a lot better than going in with a cookie cutter approach. Besides, your candidate will be impressed with your thoughtfulness and will come into the position with a deeper desire to do their best for you.

Now, once you are past all that and have agreed to the compensation package, your new candidate is ready for the next step:

The Orientation

Whatever you do, please do not underestimate this step. So many people skip on this step because they "cannot find the time," but this step is as important as any of the training you will do, if not more so.

Statistics show that people decide, on a conscious or unconscious level, how long they intend on staying with the company within the first two days on the job. A thorough and well-executed orientation process can assist the successful candidate in building their level of commitment to you and the team. Also, by how comfortable they are made to feel and by the credibility that you, your organization and your systems establish during this process.

The comfort any employee feels is directly related to their understanding of the expectations that their Managers have of them. As you can imagine, it can be very tough to deliver a winning performance if you are unsure of what that looks like. Similarly, it can be tough to make a fantastic meal for someone if you do not know what foods they love or hate or cannot eat. So while the orientation process includes things like corporate policies, cellphone usage, smoke breaks, Health & Safety, and Fire Safety Plan, all of which need to be addressed, you also want to go through the duties and responsibilities associated with their position and what the standards and expectations are. You want to help them buy into the success principles for the position that would help them achieve the results you want.

This is also where you communicate your Vision. If you can get them to buy into your Vision, and you have someone with a winning character and the determination to succeed, then all you have to do is stay out of their way. Would that not be so much more fun and rewarding than running around trying to get people to do what you need them to do?

So break it down and chat about everything on the list. Do not rush through it. Their first day on the job should not be as a contributing Team Member. The purpose of it is to help them to be familiar them with the company, the team, where to find what they need and to give them a sense of what the company is all about. So spend a couple of hours with them and introduce them to your company. It will pay back in multiples.

My process of Orientation always included my explanation of the rules, procedures, fire-safety, and regulations, but still included a full tour where I would show the new Team Member where everything is, introduce her to everyone who was there and thoroughly explain how the training process will be broken down. I even go as far as to tell to them that I will be relying on them, to some degree, to let me know how slowly or quickly they should be progressing through the various steps of training.

Take a moment before moving on to the next chapter to complete the exercises listed in this chapter.

- Create a character reference system with a space for the names and companies that you will call with the questions you want to ask. Remember to create a space for their responses, so you have a record of them. (This will help in your learning process as well).
- Set up your system for offers if one does not already exist. Remember you do not want to cookie cutter this as you may be negotiating outside of both yours and the candidate's interest.
- Set up an orientation checklist form that you can go through with the candidate during that 1st-day orientation. That will ensure you are thorough.

TRAINING AND COACHING

The goal of any training is to develop someone to the point where they operate at high performance on Auto-Pilot. We all work on Auto-Pilot to varying degrees depending on the level of comfort in our positions. The more comfortable we are in our positions, the less we think about what we are doing.

When you were a baby learning to walk you were extremely focused on putting one foot in front of the other without falling over. Once you became comfortable with it, you stopped thinking about it. Now, unless you are walking over tricky terrains like rocks or ice, you rarely ever think about walking.

In knowing that your team operates on Auto-Pilot, for the most part, it is essential to determine what level of performance are you getting and how do you elevate it? How do you take a new person and get them to the high performing Auto-Pilot stage?

Here are a few key elements in training that need to be evaluated:

- What should be done

- Why should it be done
- How it should be done
- Why it should be done that way

The WHAT, the HOW and the WHY for everything should be very clear to every Team Member

A great leader is not judged by how well his team performs when he is there, but by how well they perform when he is not. This line of thinking is directly linked to these three elements.

The first two are rudimentary and are probably followed for the most part. The third is where it tends to break down.

Tying back to your corporate and culture visions, the 'whys' should be consistent with those elements. As I have mentioned, everything you do and how it is done should be consistent with those visions.

We all do what makes sense to us. Whenever we change what we do, or how we do it, we make the change because it makes sense for us to make the change.

The law of change is that if it is not necessary to change, then it is necessary not to change.

If it ain't broke, do not fix it.

So if we are to change the 'what' or the 'how,' we have to tie it into a 'why' and show that the change is necessary. Show the difference between the results currently being achieved and the desired results.

For example, you run a restaurant, and you want to reduce your costs on cheese. Obviously, by not making any changes to procedure, you will experience no difference in results. The new system is to have all kitchen employees weigh the portions of cheese, and this is something they are not used to doing. The thing to remember is that if it does not make sense to them to weigh the cheese; they will not do it naturally. They may do it while you are watching because they know it is something you are watching for, but when you are not watching, it will not get done.

So, for the change to happen through the Process of Transition (more on that shortly), they have to buy in on the 'Why.' In this case, the "Big Picture Why" is to reduce over-portioning and build consistency in the recipe. However, that is not something the line cooks are going to get behind quickly, so this needs to be broken down to a greater degree.

Other elements that the line cooks might connect with are: fewer complaints and fewer returns to the kitchen thereby alleviating remakes; or reducing the food cost on cheese would open up the budget to buy, replace or fix some kitchen equipment that would make their job easier. In other words, what is the benefit to them? WIIFM ("What's in it for me?")

Sometimes you have to be creative, but for the most part, it is there. You just gotta sell it.

Once they buy, and it makes sense, then your job is 80% done. Then it is imperative that you become an instrument in the correction system during the Process of Transition.

The Process of Transition

The Process of Transition is the five-step process that we all go through when changing habits or behavior. The steps are:

1. Catch yourself after undesired action
2. Catch yourself during undesired action
3. Catch yourself before undesired action
4. Catch yourself thinking about undesired action
5. Free from undesired action

Here is an example I use often to describe this process:

Let's say I have a problem with interrupting people when they speak. In the first step, after I interrupt someone I would think to myself: "Crap, I just interrupted him." Now this will happen for a while. Also, interestingly enough, this is the point where most people give up. They catch themselves doing the undesired action a few times and get quite frustrated with their seeming lack of ability to get past it. After a little while of not getting it right, they quit. However, if they allowed themselves some more time to get through it they will naturally get to the next step. This process is a journey for everyone, and everyone goes at his or her own pace. So, after a little while of catching myself interrupting someone after the act, I will move on to the next step.

The next step is where I begin to catch myself in the middle of interrupting and apologize and encourage the speaker to continue. I will stay in this phase for a little while. You may find that you move through this step more quickly as the act of correcting yourself in front of other people, even if just your counterpart, is more potent that when it is all internal.

Then I begin to catch myself before I interrupt. At this point, it might be easy to think that as no one knows you were about to interrupt, it is ok to believe that you have done enough. However, as you have not reached your goal as yet, it is essential to keep going. The goal is to be wholly engaged in what the other person is saying, and at this point, we are not quite at that point.

The next step is where you will be thinking about something that you want to say. You are not about to speak or anything, but you are also not listening to the other person who is talking to you. It is important to keep focusing on ending this behavior to achieve your goal.

The final step is where you are fully engaged in what your counterpart is saying with no thoughts about what you want to say, no interrupting, but you are listening fully with the full intent on fully understanding what is being said to you.

As a side note, so many problems exist between people because we fail to listen. We jump to conclusions about what is being said to us and react, not to what is being said, but to what we think is being said.

By using the Process of Transition, I was able to move from being an interrupter to someone who is engaged and actively listening to what my counterpart is saying without thinking about it. I have essentially reprogrammed my subconscious mind on how to handle something as simple as a conversation and to do so at a higher level of efficiency.

The interesting factor to consider is that you cannot always depend on catching yourself. If you are flying on Auto-Pilot and you are not aware that you are, you will not be able to correct yourself.

What you need is the Instrument Panel in the Correction System during the Process of Transition.

Speaking of flying, a well-used analogy of correction systems is about the plane that leaves Los Angeles on the way to Hawaii. During the flight, the plane is off course 95% of the time, but because of the instrument panel that shows where it is going by course, direction, speed, and altitude, the pilot can continuously make the necessary corrections to get back on path and land in Hawaii. Moreover, once this has been programmed, this correction process can also be executed when the plane is on Auto-Pilot.

Some correction systems are incredibly efficient, and some are hit or miss. The more efficient the correction system, the quicker the change will happen.

An example of an efficient System of Correction is when you change the password on something like your smart-phone or laptop. For the first little while, you automatically punch in your old password because for you did it so long without thinking. However, what happens when you do? You do not get access to the system. Instead, the login screen pops back up prompting you to enter in the new password.

How many times do you automatically punch in the old password without thinking? How long does it take to begin to enter the new password automatically? This example highlights the process under an efficient correction system. You change quickly out of necessity.

With the example before with the cheese, it is different, because there is not an efficient system of correction. In some cases, there is no system of correction at all and so the change never actually happens. So, if you want the change to happen, you have to be an instrument in the System of Correction during the Process of Transition until it becomes automatic for the line cook to weigh the cheese.

You have to watch him and remind him each time he misses that he needs to weigh the cheese. The tighter you are on this, the quicker the change will happen. One thing I can tell you for sure, that line cook does not want you to have to keep telling him to weigh the cheese. So you catching him not weighing the cheese is what he needs to make the change happen. Also by recruiting others to be instruments of correction, the process becomes far more efficient, and while other instruments are keeping an eye on that line cook, you can divert your attention to other matters.

You do not need to yell or get angry about it. That would only serve to distract from the process of change as it has the line cook thinking more about your actions and behavior than his.

In the process of being consistent with your Vision, how you coach through the Process of Transition must also reflect your Vision. In most cases, it is best not to address what was wrong, but to only reinforce what is right.

If we factor in that only ten to twenty-five percent of what we talk about will be remembered, is not it better to spend most of the time talking about what we want and as little as possible talking about what we do not want?

By consistently reminding about what should be done, how it should be done and why it should be done, allowing the time for the Process of Transition and setting up efficient Systems of Correction, you should have no problem with training your team to Auto-Pilot high performance, even in your absence.

When it comes to monitoring your behavior, the key is first to train yourself to be aware of your actions, choices, and behavior. Develop your ability of self-evaluation to the point where you begin to do it automatically, without thinking. Allow yourself the time to go through the Process of Transition and stick with it until you get there.

By developing the habit of automatically evaluating your performance, you become an instrument in your own system of correction for yourself. This level of self-awareness will help you achieve success in all areas of your life.

In the next chapter, we will review a few techniques to consider when training for high performance in addition to the 'What,' 'How' and 'Why' format mentioned in the previous chapter. They are:

- The Puzzle Pieces
- Repeat, Repeat And Have Them Repeat Back
- Do not Overwhelm & Do not Underwhelm
- Train The Trainer & Quiz

Take a moment before moving on to the next chapter to complete the exercises listed in this chapter.

- Develop an understanding of the 'what to do's,' the 'how to do's' and the 'why's' for everything that is done in your company or department. You might even go as far as to create a binder for reference.
- Consider how you would sell the "why" to your team members to get them to buy into what needs to be done, how it should be done and to what standard.
- What kind of correction systems can you put into place in your company or organization to ensure that the right things are being done to the correct standards? How can you include others into your systems?

Marco Kelly

The Puzzle Pieces

To quote an old African proverb: "You must eat an elephant one bite at a time."

So, no matter the size of the task, you can only accomplish it in the same manner: One bite at a time.

What does this have to do with training?

Absolutely everything!

In training, the coaches and trainers must break everything down to the bite-sized pieces and feed them to the trainee only as they can digest them.

Some trainers tend to throw everything at the trainee and expect them to absorb it all and run with the ball. Moreover, then, when the trainee gets something wrong, the trainer scratches his head and says, "I'm sure I went through that in training."

How do we learn?

We evaluate and ask questions.

The challenge is that sometimes the trainee does not ask the questions out loud. They ask them inside their own heads and then try to figure the answers out themselves. And usually, but not always, they get it wrong. So it is vitally important that we fill in all the gaps.

Break it down to each element of The 'What,' the 'How' and the 'Why.' Then break them down even further to each component of those elements. Leave no stone unturned. If they say: "I know that already!" Reply with a simple: "I want to be very thorough, but because there is no way for me to know what you already know and

How To Build The Team You Want

what you do not, just let me go through everything. If you already know it, just take it as revision."

Now, let's say you have just hired a new receptionist for your office. They have been in for their orientation, and now they are ready to get their hands dirty. They need to learn what the company does, the systems that are in place, the company directory; they need to learn the ordering system (if there is one) so they can effectively direct callers to whom they need to speak to or handle any basic questions about the company. Those are some of the different elements of the position. Now, you need to break them all down even further into the puzzle pieces of office management procedures and protocols, filing systems, corporate schedules, and so on. Break it all down to individual puzzle pieces.

How do you put a puzzle together? You get all the pieces and see how they fit.

How do you know how they fit? You refer to the picture on the box.

Ah, yes! The picture on the box.

Welcome back to the Vision.

When we are training, we are giving the puzzle pieces which are the details of the processes that lead to the Vision, or 'the Picture on the Box.'

Is it that simple?

It seems so on paper, but no. It requires massive commitment on the part of the trainers and leaders to consistently reinforce the Vision through the coaching and direction of the daily duties and actions that are necessary for the processes that lead to the Vision.

In the leadership level, we call this the one thousand conversations with twenty people. Every day!

As you go through your day, consistently stopping to coach and direct, over and over again, sometimes with the same person about the same thing, you reinforce the Vision through the details of the processes that lead to it.

As things come in line, rather than direct and remind, you affirm, compliment, and celebrate with your team on the results they are getting.

Also, when we are speaking of high performing teams, we imagine that if a customer asks a new salesperson a question about a product, the salesperson can immediately answer the question and then go into detail about the features and benefits of the different products. Thus the customer is very clear about what product would be right for them based on his or her needs and applications.

What would be required in training to allow that to happen? The sales person would have had to be trained on those aspects hands-on, as well as had training materials outlining the products that they could study on their own time.

Moreover, if you have followed the recruitment processes outlined in the previous chapters, you most likely have hired the individual who would study those on his own time.

Repeat, Repeat And Have Them Repeat Back

One of the ways to evaluate problems or deficiencies is to see what the overall picture of the current state of the company looks like and compare it to a mental image of how it should look. You can be aware of any problems that exist by identifying any discrepancies between those two pictures. Then you can implement strategies and solutions to get the images to look the same. It is similar to playing that old game 'Spot the Difference.'

One of the goals as a trainer and coach is to get everyone to have the same mental picture of what 'right' looks like regarding the Vision and how it translates to the various elements of the duties in their position. If you find you are getting inconsistencies in the results you are getting from various team members, it may be due to the individual team members using incorrect mental pictures. An inaccurate mental picture would lead to wrong choices and, thus, incorrect results.

To achieve true consistency, it is essential that everyone operates from the same picture.

One way of achieving this is through repetition. Repeat over and over again the 'What,' the 'How' and the 'Why,' and repeat over and over again how it ties into the Vision. Repetition is a crucial element in learning.

Everyone can know all the words to a song and be able to sing it if they have heard it many times. If you hear a song many times, you almost automatically learn the words to that song. If you've listened to an album or compilation of music many times, as one song ends you can hear the beginning of the next song in your mind before it even starts to play. This process of training works in very much the same way. Repeat something enough times, and you will remember it. With each repetition, you will build the trainee's knowledge and understanding of what they are learning. So tell them over and over and over again. And then...

...Have them repeat back to you what you have told them.

I learned this the hard way when I found that my instructions were not being carried out as I had given them. It ties in with the idea that people only remember in the range of ten to twenty-five percent of what you tell them. Moreover, rather than ask the questions to fill in the gap, they fill them in on their own.

I learned that lesson after I had explained to someone what I needed her to do and thought to ask them to repeat back to me what I had asked them to do.

I was utterly shocked by the response I received. I had to shake my head and silently question if they were listening at all to anything I was saying.

A valuable lesson and I learned it well. Hopefully, you will too. It saves much time in going back and having to correct what they did because they filled in the gaps on their own.

Do Not Overwhelm & Do Not Underwhelm

Everyone learns at different speeds.

A quick learner going through a slow training process may get bored and de-motivated and may think: "This place is boring. I might be happier somewhere else."

A slow learner going through a quick training process may get frustrated and de-motivated and may think: "I do not think I can do this. It seems too hard. I might be better off somewhere else."

I recommend having a training process for each position regarding what is learned and how and from whom. However, be flexible on the speed of the training and tailor it to the trainee's rate of learning.

Allow the trainee to let you know when they are ready to move on. Caution them, however, to ensure they are truly prepared to go to the next phase and that in their eagerness to move on, they might be missing valuable information. Getting full value from the training before moving on is necessary, but you always want your trainee stretching and reaching, and to spend more time on something that you already have in the pocket could cause them to lose momentum.

An excellent way to determine whether someone is overwhelmed or underwhelmed is by their eyes. Now, while it may take some practice to learn to read the eyes when the signals are subtle, it will be very evident when it is at the extreme.

Underwhelmed people will occasionally roll their eyes. It may even be unconscious. This body language means: "I got it!" They may look bored and disinterested. This may be seen and misinterpreted as disinterest, which may make you think you made an error in hiring. Chances are they are being made to stay too long at a particular stage in training.

Now the stage they are on may be necessary, and they may need to stick it out despite how boring it might be. What you may need to do when you see that is to empathize with their boredom and maybe you could mention that you know it is a pretty slow part of the training, but encourage them to stick with it as there is some valuable information they will get from it that will be very helpful later.

Sometimes just being made aware that that part of the training is supposed to be boring or tough or long helps them understand that their feelings are reasonable, and then it does not lead to them second-guessing themselves or the company.

Now being overwhelmed has an entirely different set of body language clues. The left-right-left looks, the step towards one direction and then the change to another direction are usually strong indicators that the new hire is feeling a little lost. It may help in that situation to coach them it is normal to feel a little brain mush at that time, but it will pass, and they will get the hang of it soon enough.

No matter what your candidates are going through, you need to be there to hold their hands when they need it. If you are not, you might potentially damage the relationship that would usually result in performance issues. By being there, you gain more of their trust and commitment and further their direction towards being active and valuable members of the team.

Train the Trainer & Quiz

The best way of knowing for sure that your trainee is ready to move on to the next step in the trainer is to evaluate their understanding and ability of the stage they are completing.

A 'Train the Trainer' is one of the critical elements of training as it follows the principle that the best way to learn something is to teach it. The process of putting the understanding into words helps solidify the concepts in the mind of the trainee. It also helps to determine how comfortable the trainee is with that specific material and whether or not she is ready to move on to the next step.

If she demonstrates an excellent grasp of the various aspects of the material and can answer questions about the content in her own words, rather than merely regurgitate what was told to her during the training, that is a sure sign that she has it in the pocket.

If she punctuates her comments with "Um" and "Ah," then I would recommend not moving her on just yet.

Quizzes, while seeming to test knowledge, are also used as a tool to give understanding.

The questions on a quiz can be designed to feed valuable information to the trainee that you need them to know as much as test their knowledge of the material.

Example:

It is necessary to wash your hands when returning to work from using the washroom, smoking or eating:

A - To waste time before going back to work.

B - To eliminate any bacteria on the hands that could lead to food-borne illness.

C - To make sure we have running water.

D - To keep your hands from getting wrinkles.

The answer is obvious and so leads the trainee to 'guess' the correct answer in a manner that helps them remember what they should be doing.

The timing is where you can be flexible. I have trained people whom I would have to spend extra time on various steps of their training, and I have taught people whom I have fast-tracked through multiple phases. It depends on the learning ability of the trainee as well as their level of experience.

The goal is to get everyone to the same level of high performance on Auto-Pilot. The roads you take to get them there will vary. Your ability to read and evaluate and determine the right path for the right trainee will contribute significantly to the success of your training processes.

Training, in my estimation, is constant and ongoing. A high-intensity training two-week period kicks it off, but it never ends. Even for myself - I am still, and always will be, in training.

Take a moment before moving on to the next chapter to complete the exercises listed in this chapter.

- Develop a training schedule for each position. Identify what other areas they need to spend time with to understand how their job connects with the others in the company or department.
- Develop quizzes for each stage of the training schedule to use as a barometer to help you determine that they are ready to move on to the next step.
- Remember to be patient. Everyone learns at different speeds. I am usually more wary of someone who wants to jump forward in training than of someone who wants to

spend a little more time to make sure they get it right.

Think of training as an investment. The more you invest, the bigger your returns.

Evaluations

If you had a boss come up to you and say, "You know, you are doing a good job overall, but some things could be better" and then walked away, you would be left confused as to what things you needed to improve. She did not give you any specifics.

Now, in many cases, it is not as bad as that, but it is not much better either.

To adequately evaluate someone, you need to have some specifics concerning the elements of Performance and Character. A general feel for it is not enough as it provides no helpful feedback to the Team Member.

What works best is to break down the elements of Performance and Character into specifics of skills and attitudes.

One example would be to create two columns, one for each element, and begin to write down what you believe are the best attributes of each component.

I am sure you would agree that if you had an employee with every single attribute listed you would be searching for a way to clone him.

Now, with this list, you can 'grade' each employee by how well, or how poorly, each attribute describes them. The idea, or the goal, is to get each Team Member to have every single attribute with a check mark next to it. It may seem like an impossible task, and it may be, but it is one worth attempting.

With each attribute, create a thorough description of what it would look like if executed one hundred percent. For example:

Communication:

Relays relevant information as it pertains to the duties, tasks, and assignments including any obstacles or issues. Provides detailed feedback as it relates to results or impedances. Follows up to ensure relevant information has been effectively relayed and assures any further steps for continuation or rectification is documented and distributed to all parties involved.

With such a Third-Party reference, it is easy for the manager to determine if the Team Member is successfully achieving that Attribute, or if they are still facing challenges where it is concerned. The goal is to remove as much subjectivity as possible. You are looking for specific evidence from the Team Member that they are consistent and effective with the attribute. Using the above Attribute as an example, if you have a Team Member who failed to notify the Manager or relevant people regarding an issue or challenge, especially if that failure resulted in further problems being created, it is easy to say that the Team Member has not reached one hundred percent success with that particular Attribute.

By having that Third-Party reference, it makes it easy to coach and train on those specific attributes, as well as effectively evaluate without approaching it in a tentative manner. You can confidently give the score with specific examples to support your conclusion.

I always say: Shoot for the highest star, for if you miss, you will still be amongst the stars. However, if you shoot for the lowest star and miss, you might reach only the tip of a lamp-post.

Another way of looking at it is when writing an examination. Aim for 100%. If you miss, I bet that you would still do exceptionally well. If you only aim to pass and you miss; you fail!

So, with that approach, work on getting each employee to 100%.

How do you build a wall? You build it one brick at a time.

So, brick by brick, you build your team members and strengthen your team.

When you 'grade' your employees, you may find it best to do so with an "all or nothing" system. Be totally honest. What you are looking for is consistency. Having a Team Member who is engaged 80% of the time but completely disinterested the other 20% is better than having someone who is 50/50, but it is not nearly as good as having someone who is engaged 100% of the time. Be brutally honest about it.

Once you have evaluated each employee on each attribute, you will primarily be creating a list of strengths and deficiencies for them to work on. You can then coach them on the specifics of where you need them to be and set goals for one or more of the missing attributes to focus on developing before their next evaluation. It is essential also to continue to work on improving your strengths.

What you will create is continuous improvement. You want to see movement in one area or another that helps get them to be that ideal Team Member.

If they think being at 80% is good enough for you, there will be no incentive for them to get the other 20%. However, if they know that only 100% gets the checkmark, they will push themselves to get there.

When you sit to present the grades, try to use open dialogue to flush out any discrepancies between your understandings of the attributes and the Team Member's interpretation. Those dialogues will go a long way to helping the Team Member improve on those attributes. Initially, you may find that they might defend against your estimation of a missing attribute, but in using the 100% rule, even the hardest employee would be hard pressed to say they do something 100% of the time when they know they do not.

It also helps to dangle the carrot. Have an incentive in place for accomplishing specific goals. For example, if they currently have ten deficiencies, have a goal when they reduce that to seven or five. Having something to shoot for and a reward for getting it is a compelling motivator, especially when it has been broken down to specifics and is achievable.

Table of Attributes:

PERFORMANCE	CHARACTER
Attention to Detail	Amiable
Communication	Coachable
Completes Tasks	Committed
Engaged	Courteous
Focused	Helpful
Follow Up	Honesty
Follows Instructions	Listens well
Follows Procedures	Positive
Leadership	Respectful
Organized	Responsible
Preparation	Self Motivated
Productivity	Self-Control
Punctual	Supportive
Sense of Urgency	Teamwork
Timely	Tolerance/Acceptance

Be sure to balance well the affirmation of the ones they are doing well and the criticism of the ones they are missing and help them understand what the expectations are.

As much as you will be focused on helping them improve and get to the next level, be enthusiastic about the things that they are doing well and be visibly excited about the improvements they are making. If they perceive that you are only focused on the things they are doing wrong, they will not have much desire to push themselves to do better.

Approach the conversations about deficiencies with no emotion at all, like you are discussing the glossary of terms for the stock investment industry. However, when you are talking about the things they are great at and the new attributes on the yes list, be emotional, be excited, and be almost over the top about it.

When people get more attention to the good things than the wrong things, they want to do more good things. When the focus is more for the negative, what do you think happens?

Think of the little boy who is always told he is bad; he continues to be bad. And, the boy who is told he is good continues to be good. This is called labeling. Labeling is something we do all the time without even thinking about it. However, when we understand it, we can use it to our benefit. A man named David Houghton once employed me. I was working at the time at a Moneysworth & Best Shoe Repair store, and one of the policies was that the workers had to wear a branded green smock. I didn't particularly appreciate wearing that smock and many times David would come into the store and see me not wearing my smock. He never said anything about it. One day, David asked me to go to his office. He asked me to sit down and then he proceeded to tell me about one of the challenges that he was facing where some members of his team would not wear their smock. I thought I knew where this was going, and I was about to get into trouble. Au contraire, mon ami. Instead, he asked me if I would help him and be his point man to go around and make sure all his team members were wearing their smocks.

Smart man, Mr. Houghton was. I could see what he was doing, but I was so appreciative of his approach about it, that I never worked a day in that store without wearing my smock.

Rather than go on about the deficiencies, merely point them out. However, the attributes under the yes column, rave about those. I am sure you will start to see other items being added to that list.

Take a moment before moving on to the next chapter to complete the exercises listed in this chapter.

- Develop your own system of evaluating your employees using the attributes checklist. The attributes you are looking for with each position or department may differ to some degree. Spend some time thinking about what strengths, abilities, talents, skills, and actions you need for each position and create your own list. It does not need to be as long as the one I have created. You can make it simpler, or more complicated as you see fit. This is for you and your team to have a logical, almost scientific approach to evaluations where it alleviates the subjectivity of the process.
- For each attribute listed in your system, whether on the Character side of the table or the Performance side, create a reference of what it means and what is explicitly being looked for with each one. Communicate these to your team, so they know what they need to do and how to do it to be able to progress through your list and get more check-marks.

The Discipline Process

When reviewing the process of discipline, it is helpful to keep in mind what you are trying to achieve through your discipline steps and procedures. If your current disciplinary procedures are not working for you, then perhaps it is time to look at a different approach.

The goal of any disciplinary process is to inspire your team members to do their best; this can only be achieved with a fair system that offers both predictability and consistency. Your employees should always be able to predict what the consequences would be for infractions of policies or procedures, and that they would be the same no matter who the wrongdoer is. In other words, the consequences for any specific action do not change based on the mood of the one doing the disciplining, nor on which Team Member is being disciplined.

Whether it is your top guy or bottom guy committing the act, nothing should change in how it is handled.

The effectiveness of your system of discipline is best when the employees are considering their own behavior and are holding themselves accountable for it. It would not be very effective if your Team Members were being distracted from the ownership of their actions by inconsistent, unfair or erratic behavior, or in some cases a complete lack of action.

Consider the following scenarios:

Scenario 1: John comes to work ten minutes late one morning because he got a flat tire on the way to work. Julia, the manager, walks up to John and using harsh words, swearing and being generally abusive, tells John that his being late is unacceptable and if

How To Build The Team You Want

it happens again, he is fired. John is not given a chance to explain.

Scenario 2: A few minutes later, Matt also arrives late. Matt tells Julia that he is late because he had stopped to buy a cup of coffee and the service at the coffee shop was really slow. Julia says nothing and walks away.

It becomes apparent when looking at these scenarios that Julia likes Matt and has something against John. The truth is that this may not be the case, but you can certainly see how one might arrive at such a conclusion.

In the first scenario, the approach used is enough to achieve the opposite of the point of discipline. As John walks away feeling quite upset about the way he was spoken to and not being given a chance to explain, he is not thinking about how he could avoid being late again by leaving earlier and allowing himself more time. He is thinking about his manager's behavior and how it made him feel.

Then, in the second Scenario, John is even more angered and upset by how Matt's lateness was dismissed. Now he is probably thinking about finding work with another company because he can no longer respect Julia as she is a terrible manager.

Julia's management of John and Matt created negative results for both parties. She came off as unfair and insecure to John, and to Matt, she came off as weak and a push-over. Do you see how each could feel that way?

Many people use verbal warnings and written warnings as tools in their discipline steps. From my experience, they are more threats than anything as very few Managers follow through on them. It seems the Managers and leaders are as against writing up an employee as the employee is against being written up.

The reality as well, in most cases, is that the write up is only used as a tool to get rid of someone without paying them out. Not all previous misdeeds are documented until the manager has had enough and only then do they bring out the pen and paper to start documenting the misdeeds to record sufficient to justify dismissal.

I believe there is another way. A way that empowers both the manager and the employee, and which has the employee considering his own actions and not the actions of the manager. One which has him walking away from the discipline with a strong sense of what he needs to do.

This way is called A Record of Conversation.

The steps of a Record of Conversation are as follows:

1. Pre-print a clean Record of Conversation form and bring the employee's file.
2. Sit down with the employee and discuss the misdeed.
3. If not the first conversation, reiterate the comments and commitments from the previous discussion.
4. Confirm with the employee that they understand why it was wrong.
5. Confirm that they understand the policies around the action and why those policies exist.
6. Confirm with the employee their understanding of the Vision and how the policies around their action connect with the Vision.
7. Coach through dialogue on the 'WHATs,' 'HOWs' and 'WHYs.'
8. Ask them what they are committed to doing going forward.

After having this conversation, you then pull out the blank form (see fig1), write their name at the top, summarize the conversation you had regarding the action, policies, procedures, and Vision, then in the commitment section document what they said

How To Build The Team You Want

they would do from then on and have them sign it.

Having them sign it is not like with the write up where they are asked to sign off on your words about their actions. In this case, you are asking them to sign off on their own words and commitment as a demonstration of ownership of to what they have committed.

This has a potent effect as the act of signing off on something they have committed to builds a strong connection to it. If they were to go back on their words, it then becomes a question of their integrity and honesty. Documenting their own words also makes it more difficult for them to say afterward that they did not say them. It principally holds them to their own word as a matter of honor.

The point of a Record of Conversation is to help them learn from their mistakes and to empower them to push themselves to do better. Moreover, because it does not feel like negative discipline, leaders and Managers do not face the same avoidance issues with it. If the Managers can buy into the power it has in helping the employee hold themselves more accountable for their actions; it becomes something they can get behind.

In the end, should the employee be either unwilling or incapable of development and continues to perform improper actions and misdeeds, you can let them go and not worry should the labor board call to inquire about the dismissal. Since you would have many Records of Conversation where you coached them to do better, they would be satisfied. You can show that you did everything you could to help them and documented not only their understanding and acknowledgment of what was wrong and why it was wrong but also their commitment to do better.

You can fax over many pages that prove that you have done everything you can to correct the actions of the employee and have given them numerous chances to do the right thing.

So, to summarize, using the Record of Conversation with every employee with every policy or procedure infraction serves to:

- Reinforce the Vision through your approach to discipline and methods of coaching the team.
- Ensure consistency with how each employee is disciplined.
- Empower them to change by having them sign off on their own commitments.
- Document their understanding of policies and procedures.
- Assist them in connecting with the principles that are consistent with the attributes of Performance and Character.
- Create a positive team environment where the team members are focused more on what they need to do and how rather than concentrating on not doing it wrong. (Trust me; there is a massive difference in the overall energy of your team between these two focuses.)

Again, one of the critical factors is consistency. It requires commitment on your part to ensure that each time one of your team steps off the path, you coach and redirect them, have them commit to their actions moving forward and sign off on them.

Define within your system how many Records of Conversation for the same or similar infraction is allowed before taking things to the next step. Some believe in a system that offers a suspension without pay. This can work in most situations, but in some cases, people do not mind taking some extra time off. A side benefit is that if they are not happy working in your company, they would usually use this time to look for another job. Unless you want to keep them and are looking to coach and train, this would also help to solve your problem.

If you are looking to coach and inspire, what I have found to be more useful is to put them through a step in the training process again. This serves to allow them the opportunity to learn, relearn or familiarize themselves with whatever it is they are struggling. Even when the rest of the company knows that it is a positive step towards helping the Team Member get stronger, and if you have built the right culture they will be supportive and encouraging.

It can still be a bit of a blow to one's ego, however, to be put back through some of the paces. The idea as well is that your Team Members will see you as someone who is doing everything you possibly can to help that Team Member succeed and that aids in establishing your Leadership Credibility.

You will need to create a separate and different set of discipline procedures for when the employee is still within the Probationary Period. This is where you have to be diligent in consistently evaluating the progress and strengths of the employee. It is likely that they are giving you their best merely to get past probation, to a point where they feel safer, so it is vitally important that you keep a close eye on how things are going with them. Do not let someone pass probation if you feel they are not up to standard with what you need for your team. Always be open and transparent with them about what you are looking for and whether they are meeting, exceeding or coming short of your expectations. Allow them the opportunity to step up their game if they are missing the mark.

When you get close to the end of the Probation Period, and you are unsure about whether they are the right fit or not, offer them the choice between leaving on their own, or extending the probationary period. They may choose to go if they also feel that something is not clicking. Keeping them there longer might be an injustice to them as well as you. People are usually afraid to leave a position in case they cannot find another, but if they are working somewhere that is not right for them, staying there will only make them more and more unhappy and things will get worse for both the employee and the company. Stuff like that can be cancer in the culture of the company and can erode much of what you have worked so hard to build.

If, however, they request to stay and accept the extended probation, again offer them a clear and concise explanation of what you are looking for and what they need to do to show you that they are right for the team.

Marco Kelly

As we spoke about in the training process, failure to consistently correct improper behavior results in a slow or non-existent change to a team on the road to High Performance. By consistently correcting, and doing so in a manner that is empowering and positive, you will see great results.

… How To Build The Team You Want

Record of Conversation

Name: _____ Date: _____
Manager: _____ Dept:: _____

Discussion Notes

_____
_____
_____
_____
_____
_____

Committment

_____
_____
_____
_____
_____
_____

Manager's Notes

_____
_____
_____

_____
Employee's Signature

_____
Manager's Signature

Take a moment before moving on to the next chapter to complete the exercises listed in this chapter.

- Clearly define your system of discipline and list what actions result in immediate termination, what requires coaching and which actions need to be documented a certain number of times before moving on to the next stage in the discipline process.
- Clearly communicate to your team what your new coaching and disciplinary procedures are through the Orientation Process for New Hires and either through one-on-one conversations with existing team members or at a General Staff Meeting.
- Be clear that your goal is only to help each member achieve the best they can and you want to make sure they have a clear understanding of what needs to be done, how it needs to be done and why. Any discipline process is only effective when it is an integral part of the overall coaching process. There has to exist an element of consequence for when things are done wrong. You do not want to create panic and fear so that they are only focused on not doing things wrong, rather than focused on doing things right. And they need to know that you are going to do everything you can to help them succeed at the highest level. There also needs to be the understanding of what happens when someone's actions and behavior goes against the Vision and the team's and company's collective agenda.

The goal of discipline is not to punish, but to help. Not to push someone down, but to lift them up. Not to take something away from them, but to add to their understanding. It is to help them get and stay on the right track that leads to greatness: theirs and your company's.

LEADERSHIP

Despite various elements of leadership having been explained during the previous chapters, I felt it necessary to write a chapter that focuses on the aspects of leadership required for building your team and leading them to victory.

As with all teams; sports, corporate, military and other organizations, the success of the team is generally dependent on the leadership. The strength and effectiveness of the leader will dramatically impact the engagement level, the commitment, the passion, the focus, the direction and the abilities of the members of the team.

I used to say to my team: "If we succeed at this, it is because of all of you. However, if we fail, it is because of me. I say this because I firmly believe that my job is to make sure that you all have everything you need to succeed. That includes the support, the resources, the training, the inspiration and motivation as well as the right people on the team."

I took that very seriously and held myself accountable for the failures. I did not blame the failures on the members of the team or any other outside sources. I blamed myself. By doing this, when we did fail at something, I could take that as a learning opportunity to not fail that way again, and I would coach my team on that learning so we were all on the same page as to how we might take steps to avoid making those mistakes again in the future.

The story goes that when Thomas Edison was working on re-inventing the light bulb for commercial use, before his ultimate success, he had thousands of unsuccessful attempts. He made a statement that he did not fail in his efforts, but with each unsuccessful attempt, he successfully learned one more way that would not work.

Another philosophy I worked from in coaching and mentoring my teams is that if I have a problem, and I have tried everything and the problem still exists, then the problem is me. I obviously did not try everything; I just tried everything I could think of to solve the problem. So my next step was to learn more options and get more tools to try more things. When you take this approach, you begin to look at problems as challenges rather than roadblocks. By doing this, you never accept failure because to do so would be a reflection of a lack of commitment on your part to find the solution.

One of the critical elements of Leadership is that Leadership is a relationship. As Leaders, we do not choose our followers, but as followers, we choose our leaders. With that line of thinking it is natural then to assume that despite any title or position, we are not leaders unless we have inspired others to follow us.

So, again, despite title and position if we have not portrayed ourselves to our teams as being worthy of being chosen as their leader, it will not matter what we say or do, our teams will conduct themselves in accordance with their agendas, plans, and objectives and completely disregard the agenda, plan, and goals of the company and the organization.

What ensues then is chaos, all the Team Members are doing their own thing and certainly not following any Vision. Moreover, as you can imagine, it would certainly be challenging to garner success as a company if the Team Members are not working together in line with a common Vision under strong leadership. Could it be that is the main reason some companies fail? I believe so.

Without proper leadership working in conjunction with propriety, there can be no success. Propriety is defined by doing the right thing, at the right time, for the right reason, with the right people and for the right result. Propriety should be a fundamental component of your Vision.

Now some companies may operate with Leadership but without propriety, but usually they are not successful long term. Think of Crime organizations or scam companies. Usually, there is a lot of dissension and struggle within the ranks that drives things to ruin.

So how then do we inspire others to follow us?

Step 1:

It begins with a clear and concise and consistent message that is in line with a higher purpose. People want and need to make money, but they generally do not start companies just to make money. They start them to work for themselves doing something they love, and the plan is that they will make money doing it. However, the goal should never be about money. If you are doing something because you love it and it means a lot to you, the money will be there. Here is the reason why that works: if you are only doing it for the money, then on that is what you will be focused. So if you are focused on the money, what are you not paying attention to in your business? You are not paying attention to the steps that lead to success; the little things you do every day that makes a difference. However, if you are doing something important to you, something that really matters to you, you will naturally pay attention to those little things that make a difference, and success would be the natural result.

It goes back to the concept of success and process. If you have a plan for success, you cannot focus on the success; you have to focus on the plan. You have to focus on the steps that lead to success. If your goal is to be the best shoe store in your city, what is your plan to achieve that? It would revolve around the quality of the products you bring in, it would revolve around the presentation and cleanliness of your store, and it would revolve around the service you provide to your customer, and so on. So to be successful and to be the best shoe store in your city, on what should you be focused? All the factors and processes that would make that happen. You cannot just sit back and focus on success; you have to focus on the steps.

How To Build The Team You Want

Having a goal, an objective and a purpose is vital, but how do you then whittle that down to a single phrase that is memorable and relates directly to what you want to achieve?

Step 2:

Communicate that goal. When you clearly state the purpose, and how important it is, you help align your Team Member's focus and actions towards that goal. If your goal is to be the best shoe store in your city, say that! "We will be the best shoe store in this city!" If you want your department to be the highest revenue growth department in the company, then say that! If you want to be the company that makes a difference in your community, then say that!

Tell your team why you want to achieve your Vision. Share with your team the passion behind what you do and why you do it. Share with them the Vision you have for your company or department and what it means to you. And also share with them the steps that are needed to be taken to achieve that goal. With the shoe store, share with them the standards for the products to bring in, share with them how the store should look and feel, share with them the kind of experience the customers should have, leave no stone unturned. Your team should have an unambiguous picture in their minds about who you are, why you are doing what you do and how they can contribute to that.

Step 3:

Everything you do and say should demonstrate how much those goals and objectives mean to you. You cannot show your team a road, tell them that road is the one we must go down, and then take a different road yourself. How can they follow you on the path you have shown them if you are not leading them down that path?

Everything you do and say should show your commitment to the Vision you have shared. You cannot sit back and relax now. You are in the game, and you are pushing hard; you are the Quarterback and the Cheerleader.

Is that all? Not quite.

It also comes down to your character. You must earn the trust of your teams, and you can only do this by demonstrating key aspects consistent with a strong and good character.

As with the attributes of Performance and Character as defined in Chapter 9: Evaluations, the same thing applies to Leadership and you can use these to evaluate your own Performance and Character when it comes down to leadership. Rather than set them up in the type of template we used for employee evaluations, it is better to look at them with a deeper perspective as you would do with your employees when going through the attributes during actual evaluations.

What does integrity mean? Some people have an incorrect idea of the definition of integrity. Some people believe that it is operating within a general set of values or principles. This is only somewhat true. A more accurate description is: You operate within your specific set of principles or values. Simply, it means your actions and behavior is consistent with your values and beliefs. The emphasis here is on the 'your.'

Our philosophies are the guiding principles with which we navigate our way through life. They also happen to be the same set of principles by which we judge others. We have a set of beliefs about how the world works, and we expect others to live by those beliefs, but the truth is that we all have our own. There are, however, a set of principles that we are expected to demonstrate as leaders and in the following Chapter, The Leadership Tool Box, I will touch on a few of them. Principles that if demonstrated consistently will make all the difference in being able to build your team and lead them to victory.

THE LEADERSHIP PROFILE

The Leadership Profile is a set of character traits that we look for in our leaders. I have always found it intriguing that some people can demand specific characteristics in others and have certain expectations about how others should conduct themselves, but not demand those same traits from themselves.

As a process of inspiring others to follow us, it helps to understand what we look for in others whom we might choose as a Leader, and then learn to emulate them consistently until they become second nature. It helps if you use the Process of Transition as described in Chapter 4: Training & Coaching

As you read each one, think about how it currently fits with you and whether you could do better.

The first valuable and necessary attribute of being an effective and strong leader is being of good character. You will only be viewed and valued as a leader to the level of the strength of your character. Creating a Vision and building a plan around that Vision is necessary, but it would be tantamount to designing a wall and designing the plans to build it, but using inferior materials in the construction. The wall would not be secure regardless of how well planned or even how well it is made. If the materials used are flawed, then the whole wall is defective.

This means that if you are honorable, ethical, loyal, patient, trustworthy, operates with integrity and your actions, behavior, and your words are consistent with these attributes, then your team members will feel comfortable in choosing you as their leader and will follow you to the end of the earth.

Genuine Care

Did you notice in the previous Chapter that I said 'choose you as their leader?' Also, that Leadership is a relationship? We do not choose our followers; we choose our leaders. Regardless of your position or title, you are not a leader until someone decides you are their leader.

Effective leaders understand this principle, and they know that their job as a leader is to inspire others to choose them as leaders so they can influence and direct. If you are not selected as a leader by the members of the team you are supposed to lead; you will have no influence. We inspire others to choose us as a leader by demonstrating genuine care for their well being and their success. If your team members believe that you will break through walls for them and have the power to do so, they will want to break through barriers for you. If they think, however, that you do not care about them, but only yourself, they will not care about you either. That is the Law of Reciprocity.

The point in this is that you cannot pretend to care about them to try to inspire them to choose you as their leader. The reality is that they will see through it and not trust you at all. Sometimes they will not even know why they do not believe you, but they will feel that something is not right. You have to care about people if you are going to succeed as a leader of people. If you do not care about people, you might want to consider a different role for yourself and let someone else be the leader of your organization.

Decisive

As a leader, it is necessary for you to be decisive. Things are going to come up and you are not always going to know how to deal with them. However, you have to have a system in place to evaluate the situation, list the possibilities of how to handle the situation and make a decision as to which way to go. This can sometimes be something as simple as calling a meeting of the minds with your team, or with a selected committee relating to that type of event, and opening the forum for discussion with your team to develop and implement a solution. If, however, you appear beaten, lost, confused or in any way unsure of yourself, you will lose valuable points of credibility as a leader. So, in line with your Vision, implement a system of how decisions are made and what processes are used to make them. This way, no matter what comes at you; your decisiveness is in putting into action the system you have designed to deal with those types of occurrences.

The other benefits of the team or committee approach to problem-solving are:

People are more apt to go along with something they helped create than what was communicated down to them.

You are empowering your teams or committees to learn how to think about problem-solving, and that inspires ownership thinking.

You are strengthening the bonds and the commitments of your team to your company or department.

There may be times when you just need to make a decision. There are three questions you can ask yourself to help you determine

How To Build The Team You Want

the right course of action:

Will this choice benefit the customers? Will this choice benefit the Team? Will this choice benefit the company? If you can answer yes to those questions, then you know you have the right answer. If the answer is no for any of them, then you still have some work to do. Remember propriety.

Being decisive does not mean that you have to decide quickly; it just means you have to make a decision. You can't sit on the fence and get comfortable; you have to choose a path.

Another excellent strategy for decisiveness is to always think in terms of the outcome. When you are faced with having to make a decision, consider what the best possible outcome would be and then work backward. You can also train your team to do this on consensus decision. You could even begin the meeting with your team when deciding a group by asking: "What is the best possible outcome we could achieve from this?"

Balanced

Being balanced means being fair. It also means being even-keeled.

Being fair is essential when dealing with your team because if they believe you always to be fair, they are more likely to trust your decisions, even when it might impact them a little negatively. They will know that you are doing the right thing because you always do the right thing.

When you are consistently fair-minded and right-minded, it also helps you develop more influence with your team.

The even-keeled aspect is an often overlooked one. I was watching an episode of the Dog Whisperer with Cesar Milan a little while ago. In the episode, the issue with the dog was relating back to the emotional and sometimes physical outbursts from the dog's owner. The owner was frustrated that the dog would not listen to him, but his behavior with the dog is what was perpetuating that situation. Cesar explained to him that if you appear to be emotionally unstable, the dog will not choose you as his leader. I thought about that a lot and realized it related to people as well. When you appear emotionally unstable to your team, they will not trust you and therefore not choose you as their leader.

Examples of emotional instability are yelling, screaming, storming around, throwing things, banging things, slamming doors, swearing, and so on.

However, when you are always calm and self-assured, no matter what crap may be hitting the fan that day, your team will always look to you to show them or tell them what to do.

Think of a sea captain on a ship that has just hit an iceberg. If he starts panicking and running around emotionally unstable, how will his crew react? However, if he remains calm and self-assured, his team will look to him to tell them what to do, and he is more likely to get the situation under control and create a positive outcome. The other way, it is more likely that everyone will start throwing themselves overboard.

Being balanced does also mean being fair. The scales of justice are always aligned. You can't have rules for some people that don't apply to all. This can be a challenge sometimes, as you may have a team member come to you to ask you to allow them to do something that is against the rules or policy. For you to enable that person to bend the rules, it will open the doors to chaos as other people will look to also bend that rule, and maybe different rules as well.

If you find that a rule no longer requires being in place, then remove it, or change it. Don't do it on a whim, really evaluate it, but if deemed to be no longer valid, get rid of it.

There is a term in business called the Sacred Cow. This refers to an idea or system that may have at one time been necessary but is no longer. An example of this might be having a rule that states all employees must ensure that the ashtrays at their desk will need to be emptied and washed every night. Well, obviously no one smokes at their desk anymore, so it is silly to have that rule.

Sometimes in companies can have all kinds of Sacred Cows and never realize it. You might ask someone why something is done a certain way, and the answer you get is "because that is the way we have always done it."

One of my favorite stories is of the little girl who asked her mother why she cut the ends off of the ham when she was cooking it. She replied, "I don't know; that was the way my mother cooked it." The little girl went to her Grandmother and asked her why she cut the ends off the ham. Her grandmother replied, "I don't know, that was the way my mother cooked it." Then the little girl went to her great-grandmother and asked her the same question. Her great-grandmother looked at the little girl and said matter-of-factly, "Because my pan was too small."

Balance is a quest for all areas of life. Remember that having problems is not a problem; it is the way of it all. Some people get so hung up on the idea that they have problems that instead of focusing on solving the problems, they just go around complaining about the problems they have. As with balance, there are ups and downs, good times and bad, high times and low, and through it all, you have to roll with the punches and keep your keel even in the water so you can keep on course. It is not easy, in fact, sometimes it is downright difficult, but only through steering through the turbulent waters can you come out on the other end to the calm.

Empowering

As you can imagine, it would be challenging to trust a leader who does not have knowledge of the organization and the details of the operation. Being able to have conversations with your team, and to be able to coach them in the right direction when they hit walls, is crucial for establishing credibility with your team. Does that mean if you hire engineers that you need to know more about engineering than they do? Not at all, but you should know what results they should be producing and be thorough in reading your reports to know if they are on pace, or if there are any deficiencies or issues.

Although I believe you need to be able to identify problems and coach your team members through them, I do not believe in micromanaging. I think that you have to paint the picture, set the course and let them utilize their talents, the ones you pay for, to produce the desired outcomes that contribute to the overall success. Problems arise, however, but rather than you tell them how to fix it, empower them to tell you how it should be fixed. You may already know the answer, but if you tell them, rather than lead them through the thinking process to come up with the right answer, they will not learn how to think about the solutions and will always be looking for you to solve the problems.

You might think this is a good thing. You might be the type that believes that for something to be done right you have to do it yourself, but I'm here to tell you that this line of thinking is flawed. You are better off teaching your team on how to think and approach problems and how to come up with solutions that are in line with the Vision and goals of the company. Otherwise, you are creating a mountain of work and responsibility for yourself, and aren't the members of your team there to help you, not to add more work? Also, what if something happens to you? What happens to your company or department then? What if you cannot be there? Does everything fall apart without you? Alternatively, have you led your team so well that they have everything under control and things continue at the same high level despite your absence? You are their leader, and they need your energy and Vision and encouragement and to celebrate the wins with them, but they do not require you telling them how to do the jobs you have hired them to do. Not after you have recruited well, trained expertly and empowered them to push themselves to excellence.

Some might get a sense of importance or significance in thinking that things would fall apart without them. However, the reality is, if things would fall apart without you, then you have failed miserably at the task of building a team and leading them to victory. The only thing you would have built is your own ego and a team of people who are certainly not empowered. I guarantee you that an empowered, motivated team would beat a micromanaged team hands down.

How much better would it be for you to go on vacation with your family without any worries whatsoever about what you will be walking back into on your return? I can tell you from first-hand experience the stress of being away and continually worrying about what is happening with the company. I can also tell you that it is not fun, being able to relax and knowing that everything is going to be taken care of is so much better. Moreover, this can only be accomplished by learning to delegate and by coaching and empowering your team to function at the high level you have set for them.

Flexible

Some view flexibility in leadership as a weakness. Some believe you must be rigid in your thinking and leadership style. Quite the opposite is true. Also, when you become rigid in your leadership style, flexibility with standards is generally the result.

A great leader is flexible in his or her style and adapts their method of communication to the personalities of their team members. A great leader is also rigid on the standards.

There are four main types of personalities, and each one has a different way of communicating. Without getting too deep into it, here is a brief overview:

1. Extrovert – Assertive and People-Focused
2. Pragmatic – Assertive and Task-Focused
3. Amiable – Passive and People-Focused
4. Analytic – Passive and Task-Focused

When I think of an extrovert, I think of a cheerleader; fun, friendly, warm and inviting. Generally disorganized because the task of organizing things is tedious, they would much rather be entertaining. Their communication style is open, direct and they want stories, they want to be entertained. They are quick to make a decision.

When I think of a Pragmatic, I think of a business leader in a suit. Cool, calm, neat and organized. They do not want to hear stories; they want enough information to make a decision and no more. Moreover, they will make the decision quickly.

When I think of an Amiable, I think of a Peacemaker, gentle, people loving person, warm and friendly in a comforting and encouraging manner. They like stories and want you to paint a picture with words for them. You might give them all the information they ask for and more, and it seems as if they are ready to make a decision, but they will take their time.

When I think of an Analytic, I think of an Accountant. Usually has all the technology working for them. They do not want stories, and they do not want the numbers rounded up or down. They will analyze everything many times to make the right decision and so takes some time before concluding.

A Leader who understands the different personality types would realize that if he is speaking to everyone in the same manner, a manner consistent with his own personality style, then he would naturally only be connecting with people who share his personality style. By changing your communication style to match the personality of the Team Member you are talking to, you are more likely to be able to connect with everyone on your team, and they will feel closer to you because, after all, birds of a feather flock together. Moreover, if you can change your feathers, you can get along with all the birds.

I encourage you to learn more about personality styles to develop this skill. It will serve you greatly in your leadership endeavors.

Being rigid in your line of thinking can impede your ability to change course when it becomes evident that the company is going in the wrong direction. Being rigid could also make it impossible for you even to see that the company is going in the wrong direction. Remember humankind's biggest addiction? Never make a decision without looking at things from every angle and exploring all options, but when a decision is made, and it appears to be the wrong one, waste no time in making the changes necessary.

Some leaders let their ego get in the way and stay the course they have set even though it appears to be the wrong one. Maybe they think they will lose face with their teams if they make changes and go back on their decision. Quite the opposite is true. If you stay the wrong course, and your team knows it is the wrong course and you do not take the action necessary to get on the right path, you will lose the faith of your team.

When it comes to standards, however, this is where you are to be rigid. Set high standards and refuse to compromise on them. And, in the immortal words of Jim Sullivan, 'what you permit, you promote.'

If you allow something to happen that is against the standards or rules of your company and Vision, then the message you send is that you are not committed to the standards or rules of your company and Vision. Moreover, whatever it is will continue because you have sent the message that it is ok.

By being rigid with your standards and holding everyone, including yourself, to those standards, you develop a consistent set of values within your organization that everyone adopts as the principles by which they govern themselves. It is also easier to maintain those standards if they are consistently enforced as opposed to the ambiguity and confusion that is created when they are only sometimes implemented.

Evolving

What do I mean by evolving? As Harry S Truman stated, "Not all readers are leaders, but all leaders are readers."

Leaders are always on the lookout for more tools, more ideas, more techniques, better understandings. Just as you are reading this book, you are looking to evolve.

Leaders who are committed to growth and evolution also inspire this in their team members. A team that is made up of people seeking their own individual growth, as well as their collective growth, is an unstoppable team.

Always be on the lookout for more information that you can use to view, analyze, evaluate, and make decisions. It will only make you better, stronger, faster and smarter, and who does not want that?

Socrates wrote, "Employ your time in improving yourself by other men's writings so that you shall come easily by what others have labored hard for."

The fact that you have this book in your hands means that you already subscribe to this line of thinking to some degree. I applaud you. Not for buying my book, that would be brash, but for buying a book to help you grow and develop and evolve.

It is through a consistent and robust commitment to personal growth and development that amazing things are achieved.

Another of my favorite quotes is from Eric Hoffer: "In times of change the learners shall inherit the earth, while the learned find themselves beautifully equipped to deal with a world that no longer exists."

Marco Kelly

Honesty and Your Word

Nothing could damage your reputation more as a leader than to have your honesty in question. You may have, in your life, been working for someone whom you felt had lied to you, or promised things that they never were going to deliver on. How did you think of them as a leader? I guess that you did not think of them as a Leader at all.

It is very easy to lose faith in someone you feel you cannot trust and there are many things that you can do, without even thinking about it, that can make people lose trust in you.

Many years ago I was working at a restaurant in Edmonton, Alberta. I worked in the kitchen during the day and tended bar at night. The manager there promised me that if I proved myself, he would begin the process of cross training me in preparation for Management training.

My goal was to be a Manager, but that didn't drive me as much as my desire to do my best. I had an inherent sense of pride in my work and tried to do the best I could with everything I did.

The company had strict policies about paying over-time, so they would keep a diligent eye on everyone's time card and anyone who hit the eight-hour mark for the day was told they could go. Because I ran the line for lunch and then came back to work the bar at night, this would happen to me quite frequently. On busy nights I would get the scissors gesture from the Manager indicating I was 'cut,' meaning I need to go. The challenge was that I had not finished getting my bar back in shape. I needed to pack beer, clean the slush machine, wipe down the bottles, wipe down all the surfaces and sweep and mop the floor.

Moreover, I certainly could not leave it for someone else to do. I have always believed that your work is an ambassador of your character. I could not leave the bar in a mess, so I would clock out and continue to work until the bar was once again in tip-top shape.

Many times the manager would insist I leave, but he soon gave up that battle as he grew to learn that I could not go until the job was done.

In addition to all of that, any time I was called to cover a shift, I would come in, despite my wife's anger and objections. Sometimes it was for the bar, sometimes to work on the line; sometimes it was for prep, there were even times when I would come in to wash dishes.

In my mind, I was proving myself. I was loyal, hard-working, always available to help and diligent about my work. The promise of cross training or getting into the Management program was never brought up. Someone once said that they wouldn't move me because I was too valuable where I was, and they would have to hire two or three people to cover what I did. I think it was supposed to flatter me or make me feel better for not being recognized. All I saw was that a promise was made and not delivered.

In looking back, I realized that there might have been something that I was failing to demonstrate that resulted in not being moved into the Management program. However, I also understand a couple of other things. The bar that had been set was too vague. "Prove yourself." What did that mean exactly? Also, there was a failure to communicate what my deficiencies were so that I could work on them. It was easy to see that I was committed and would be open for direction.

Needless to say, I went and found work elsewhere. I worked both jobs for a while but had some substantial time issues. The two companies were on opposite sides of the city and getting from one job to the other in time was sometimes a challenge. I worked the other job from 6 AM to 3 PM and started work at the first restaurant at 4 PM.

I was late quite a few times, and they cut me some slack, but after a while they let me go. They put up with my tardiness for a lot longer than I expected, probably due to my level of performance up to that point, but in the end, they did what they had to do. What kind of message would they be sending to the rest of the team if they didn't? However, I have to say that by then, I no longer cared. Maybe it was them realizing that I no longer cared that resulted in them finally cutting the chord.

One of the most significant factors that reveal your real character is how you live by your word. When you promise something, and you stick by it even when you don't want to, it says a lot about you. When you promise something and flake out, that says a lot about you too.

In the old days, you would hear people talk about their name. The honor and importance of a person's name was earned through integrity and living by your word. That was a time when contracts were not written in pen but by a firm grip of a handshake. If you said it, you meant it, and you lived by that. If you said you would do something, you did it no matter what.

Those days are long gone. We need written contracts now because some people do not share that sense of honor and integrity. However, the reality is as a leader you are writing contracts with your team every day in words, words of intent, and words of promise, words in exchange for effort, passion, and focus. In addition to the employment contract where it says you will pay them for their time, we have verbal agreements where you inspire and motivate them to perform at a high level in exchange for recognition, reward, importance, praise, and affirmation.

If you fail to deliver on your part, the result may be that members of your team stop caring and no longer perform at a high level. You may then question their commitment and challenge them;

you might threaten them that if they don't get their act together that you will dismiss them. It might all escalate into some big problem, all because you didn't live by your word.

Be honest about your expectations and be honest in your feedback as well. Be diplomatic when you need to be, being tentative when you need to be, but always be honest. It is the only way to really build trust with your team.

Inspire

How do we inspire others?

As we deal with our teams, sometimes they will feel beaten or tired. Sometimes they might lose hope of achieving the Vision and the goals. It is not always easy, and the hardest part is at the beginning when the going is tough. It gets easier when you build some momentum, but it can be draining when you do not see the results from your efforts.

Sometimes you need to have patience. Sometimes it is tough to be patient. That is when your team looks to you for inspiration. It is like they are knocking on your door on Halloween night with an empty pillowcase saying "Trick or treat!"

Here is where you have to deliver. Here is where you have to fill up their pillowcase with hope and determination and fight. If you allow it to remain empty it will get discarded and with it their commitment to you and your company. The proverbial 'throwing the baby out with the bathwater.'

So what do you do?

Give them hope. Repaint the picture of where your team is going and what you have to do to get there. Talk about what they have achieved so far. Talk about how far they have come. Repeat the goals and the steps and repeat how by keeping focused on those steps the results will come.

Paint pictures with words like:

"If you take a battering ram against a wall long enough, the wall has to come down!" Some things just take time.

Be confident. Trust in yourself that you will make any necessary

How To Build The Team You Want

changes and evaluate all plans and strategies to determine that you are doing everything you possibly can to make it happen.

Above all, do not be annoyed by their worry that things are not happening as expected. Their worry is a sign that they care, that they are committed. Praise them for their worry and thank them for their concern.

They need positive energy; they need a burst of enthusiasm. They need to know that they are still in the fight and that you are there fighting alongside them. Remember that old quote: "It is not the size of the dog in the fight; it is the size of the fight in the dog.

I remember leading a team at an upscale restaurant in Toronto, and we were looking at a huge turn-around. We were rebuilding the brand of the restaurant, and we were faced with a mountain of doubt.

I presented my business case to the General Manager of the hotel outlining what I wanted to do and what it was going to cost. We identified our new breakeven point, and I set myself to the task of making it happen with my team.

We set our goals, and we started working towards them. We passed the first milestone and the next, and we celebrated. We had surpassed even our own expectations of how successful we would be.

Afterward, during conversations with members of my team, I learned from them that what inspired them was that I never spoke of what-if's as in 'what if this doesn't work' or 'what if we can't make it happen.' It was never even considered that we wouldn't do it.

They were also inspired by the way I never lowered my expectations of them. I told them I believed we could do it to the highest level. They believed I believed it, and I did. What mattered is that I never stopped pushing them to be the best. I kept at them to perform their duties and tasks to the highest standards possible. I never relinquished, I never backed down, and I just kept pushing. I pushed them further than they thought they could go and I never let up. There was no compromise. No retreat, no surrender. We had set our goals, and I wasn't quitting until we succeeded.

I never pushed negatively; I just demanded the best from them and was there to lavish praise when they delivered. There were times when I was very tough. One evening my wife accompanied me to a special event at the restaurant, and she witnessed how I worked with my team. She said to me afterward that she could never work for me. I was surprised by this, and I asked her why? She said because I was too tough and relentless. Maybe it was an outsider's perspective, but I know my team loved and respected me and together, as a Team, we achieved amazing things.

I was tough but fair. I was relentless, but always positive. The main reason that I was so effective, however, was that I was consistent. I was always the same guy. I wasn't happy and friendly and familiar one day and screaming and yelling the next. I was always the same guy, pushing and celebrating. Encouraging, rewarding and demanding nothing but the best.

I learned afterward that what inspired them the most was seeing it come together and watching the progress that we were making and knowing that if we keep pushing it will only get better.

There have been times when I did not succeed. I learned from them. In the scenario I just described, I know why I succeeded, and I learned from that as well. I knew I had to keep inspiring to make the miracles happen, so I did.

THE LEADERSHIP TOOL BOX

There are going to be times when you will inherit team members or even full teams. They will be people that you did not select, and whom you may not have selected if given a choice. Sometimes you are going to be working with team members that you cannot dismiss, and who know it, and who will challenge you because they think there is nothing you can do to them. There may also be times when you will have team members whom you did select that may challenge you.

People are slaves to their emotions for the most part, and sometimes the emotions run high, and this leads people to make decisions that they would not usually make while in a logical, rational, calm mental state. How you respond to their actions can either serve to further validate your leadership, or erode it completely.

Different problems will arise, different emotional reactions and numerous confrontations, all serving to test your leadership skills and strength. The goal is to have the tools to deal with whatever comes your way. Confidence comes from the knowledge that you are capable of dealing well with whatever situation you are faced. No matter what happens, you trust that you will be able to deal with it and create the best outcome. However, the only way you can do that is if you have all the tools available.

The more tools you have in your toolbox, the better equipped you are to face any challenge. The comfort in believing that you would know what to do, or be able to figure out what to do, in the various situations gives you high confidence as a leader. The demonstration of confidence can do much for you as people are more likely to follow someone with confidence than someone unsure of himself.

As we mentioned before, many tend to become rigid in their leadership style. This is due in large part to that leader only having a few tools in their belt. So, when approaching a situation they do not have the right tool for they end up handling it poorly or not at all. Either way, wrong messages are sent, and the result is an erosion of influence or a compromise on standards. Remember, what you permit you promote, so if you are faced with an issue that needs to be addressed and you fail to do so, you are sending the message that that issue is now part of the norm.

The following is a list of various approaches to challenges. We can look at these as having the multiple tools in your tool belt, and you can pull out the right tool for the job as you need it. It would be hard to build anything without the right tools, would it not?

Dragnet Beginning

It is important to remember that whenever you address an issue with your team members, do not introduce conclusions or judgments first. There was a TV show that ran from 1951 to 1959 called Dragnet. In the show, the main character Sergeant Joe Friday was a Las Angeles Police Detective. When questioning a witness, while relaying their story of the events he kept them on point by repeating "All we want are the facts, Ma'am" It later went on to be parodied in many ways and eventually shortened to "Just the facts, Ma'am." I like the shortened version as it is easier to connect to and remember. Just the facts!

Begin all of your approaches with this in mind. Begin with the facts. It is hard to argue with facts. Remember though, to separate your story and conclusions from the facts themselves and stick to just the facts. For example, if someone was rude to a customer it may be natural to conclude that they do not care about that customer; however, the fact in the situation is not that they do not care. The 'fact' is that they behaved in a manner that is not consistent with the Vision; they treated a customer in a way that is deemed unacceptable. Begin with that fact; then you can talk about the natural conclusion you arrive at based on the facts, i.e., they do not care. From that allow them to help you understand better why they behaved the way they did. Remember also, the story you tell yourself about the facts, may not be the right story. Seek first to fully understand the situation by stating "Just the facts" then on to how you perceive that, and then open dialogue for more significant discussion.

The benefit of this approach is that your team will view you as being open and understanding and you begin to build trust with your team. It also has them never feeling attacked and defensive, which keeps things open for great dialogue, and also, you have them beginning to pay more attention to their own behavior and how it connects to the Vision.

Parental Approach

There will be times when someone on your team requires a little one-on-one hand-holding to get through a phase or stage of training. I see this as parallel with sitting down with your child to really help them understand and connect to the bigger picture.

I had a guy, let's call him John, who used to work for me. John was one of those types of people who would push the envelope to see what he could get away with. He adopted the philosophy that it is better to ask forgiveness than permission. Sometimes John would forge ahead and do something that he might not be allowed to do had he asked.

Now, this approach can be a good thing so long as all the right things are considered. The other thing with John was that he was terrific with customers. They just loved him. Also, he enjoyed taking care of them.

So, the challenge with John was that he would sometimes make decisions on behalf of a customer, or sometimes himself, that was not always in the best interest of the company. There were many things I had to consider when deciding how to coach John including not crushing his spirit, encouraging his relationships with customers, not damaging our long term relationship, empowering him to make decisions and helping him develop the systems and tools to be able to look at the big picture. I would be using the same approach that I would use with my son if I were helping him make decisions in his life. I don't want to make his decisions for him or tell him what would be the right thing to do. I want to help him see the big picture so he can learn to make those right decisions for himself.

I definitely could not go in there charging and laying down the law as that would surely drive him away. So, I knew I had to approach it gently and help John be able to make the connections between actions and outcomes, cause and effect. I invited him to sit with me at a table, and we had a lengthy dialogue about what the overall goals and objectives were for the company and how they connected with his personal goals and objectives. I had to have many conversations with John and repeatedly painted and repainted the picture for him to understand the bigger purpose, all the while softly and gently injecting philosophies around positive character attributes like integrity, honesty, respect, courtesy, and so on.

After a while, I began noticing a real change in John, and although there were still a few challenges, there was a definite and dramatic difference in his overall approach to the duties and tasks of his position. Months later, he went on to bigger and better things and sent me a note thanking me and saying that it was because of all that I had taught him that he was able to land his new role. I explained to him that it was all on him because he was open and receptive to the coaching and that made all the difference.

The reason I call this the Parental Approach is that it is a softer, gentler approach that takes into consideration the impacts on the long term relationship. It starts with the heart and focuses on helping the other realize the bigger picture and to make better decisions to navigate their way through to achieve the desired outcomes. Same as I would for my kids.

So, when you are faced with a Team Member who is struggling with some aspects of their role, especially where it pertains to character, and you recognize that taking a tough approach will negatively impact the relationship, think of the Parental Approach. Take the time to spend some one-on-one coaching time with your Team Member to help them cultivate new beliefs and philosophies that will help shape the choices they make.

Directive Approach

This is one of the most common forms of Leadership in companies. It is an approach that should not be used much, not nearly as much as it is. There are, however, times when this approach is necessary.

I remember reading a book when I was much younger called "The One Minute Manager" by Kenneth Blanchard. It was an amazing book and I learned so much from it. It was the book that began my journey of learning about leadership. This book was written thirty years ago as I write this, and is as relevant today as it was then. In this book, however, I had an issue with a certain way of doing things. The book taught about One Minute Appraisals and One Minute Reprimands. And, although I had learned to use those techniques during the times I could get my team member aside for a minute, and they were and are powerful techniques that still work, I did not always have a minute, so I sometimes needed to utilize the directive approach and give quick instructions.

I would have follow-up conversations at the end of the shift to either clarify a point or explain the reason for the Directives I gave them. I was always taught that reprimands should be done at the end of their shift or the beginning of their next. Some might say never to do a reprimand at the beginning of a shift as it puts the person in a negative state of mind and this would impact their ability to perform their duties in the best manner. If you still think that, go back and read the chapter: The Discipline Process where I talk about the Record of Conversation. Whenever I used this approach to address an issue, the team member usually left the meeting feeling empowered and energized rather than deflated and beaten up.

However, let us get back to the Directive Approach. There are times when you need to communicate a plan that needs to be executed immediately, no delay, and no time to explain. Something happens that needs to be reacted to quickly that involves other people. Sometimes you just have to instruct and direct to get things done. You can always explain it later.

If you use this approach unnecessarily and too often, people will grow resentful. You might be perceived as a power-tripper. They would begin to think of you as a weak manager, rather than a strong leader. This, incidentally, is the opposite of how people overusing that approach believe they are being perceived.

In this approach, you issue orders; Orders that need to be carried out immediately. If they do not need to be done immediately, do not use this approach. Instead, use an approach that allows you to help them fully understand what needs to be done, how it needs to be done and why it needs to be done.

In this approach mainly, as it can easily be perceived as a negative approach, it is imperative that it not be used in a harsh manner. Just because you are issuing an order, it does not mean that it needs to be done rudely or abruptly. You can still speak to your team with respect while instructing them to carry out a task or assigning them a specific duty to attend to immediately. You still need them to trust you and disrespectfully speaking to them can go a long way towards losing their trust.

Confrontational Approach

It is funny how many people seem to have an issue with confrontation and view it as a negative thing. They avoid it at all costs until they have been stretched to the limit and then come out swinging. I believe it is better to have many small confrontations with the right approach than to have one big battle with a large scoop of anger sprinkled with frustration. In this Approach we use confrontation in the definition of 'face-to-face,' to present feedback, to offer constructive criticism, or to face a difficult situation and deal with it without avoiding it.

I was working for a Hotel as the Assistant Food and Beverage Manager many years ago. I arrived at work for my evening shift and to relieve the Food and Beverage Supervisor from the day shift. While we were going through the day's events, she told me about an issue with one of the servers that day who was not doing his job. I asked the supervisor how she handled it, and she told me that she was not in the mood to deal with it, so she didn't say anything to the server. I could not believe it. I told her she did not have the luxury of not dealing with it. "I can appreciate it if you were angry and needed a few moments to compose yourself, but it cannot be ignored or dismissed without attention. " I also asked her how she could complain to me about the Server not doing his job and then relate how she did not do hers either.

So, in that example, you can see how I used the confrontational approach to help her understand the big picture, but also how she failed to use the confrontational approach and did not address a concern with a Team Member regarding his performance. As you may remember, what you permit, you promote.

You always have to address the issues. Sometimes you need to walk away and come back if you recognize that you or the person you need to coach is in the wrong mental state, but it still needs to be done.

One of the ways I used to set this up with my Teams is by telling them the Maurin Story as part of the first General Staff Meeting I have with the team and as part of the Orientation Process with each new Team Member.

The Maurin Story:

I was working as a Server in a restaurant many years ago. It was an upscale restaurant where the tables were set with many pieces of cutlery. Main fork, Appetizer fork, Main knife, Soup Spoon, Dessert Fork, Dessert spoon, Teaspoon, Butter knife, etc. It was part of our job to maintain the table with the proper cutlery. If a table did not order appetizers or Soup, we were to take the unneeded cutlery away. If a customer ordered a steak, we were to take away the Main knife and "Mis En Place" a steak knife, etc. (Mis En Place is a French term used in the industry that means Everything In It is Place.)

I worked with a girl whose name was Maurin. Maurin was from Mexico. She was lovely, smart, genuine and gorgeous but she had the personality of a pit bull when something was wrong.

It was either my first or second day at this restaurant, and I had forgotten to follow one of the steps of Mis En Place at one of my tables, and after she had run some food to them, she noticed my error and came up to me to point it out rather bluntly. I was a bit taken aback by her approach and thought in my head was: "Who are you and why are you in my face?" Maurin was another Server and not in a position of authority, so I was a little resentful of her approach. I did not say anything, but went and took care of what I needed to.

This happened again a couple of nights later, and again I was taken aback by her approach and thinking "Who are you and why are you in my face?" Again I said nothing but went to do what I had to do.

The third time it happened I was about to say something to Maurin to the effect of "Get out of my face!" although likely using more colorful language than that. However, as I was about to deliver these words, something clicked in my brain. I stopped myself, genuinely thanked Maurin for her input and went to do what I needed to do.

The thing that clicked in my brain was the realization that if for no other reason than to keep Maurin out of my face, I would be better at my job. I was genuinely thankful to Maurin. She created within me the need to be more focused and attentive to the details of my job. This increased my performance. In the end, I became more appreciative of Maurin, and we became pretty good friends. As I got to know her better, I realized how amazing she was. An experience I would have greatly missed out on had I reacted the way I was initially going to. I am grateful I was able to catch myself and had that click in my brain. I learned a lot from that situation.

As part of my telling that story to my Team, I tell them to perceive me like Maurin and that when I am on them, it is only because I want them to do well and perform at the highest level. I would go on to explain that as long as I am on them to do things, it is because I believe they can do it. I tell them not to worry when I am on them, but to worry when I'm not. "If I am not on you to do things," I would say, "It may be because I do not believe in you anymore. That is when you worry." It was a funny moment when I had a Team Member come to me and ask if I still believed in her. She mentioned I had not coached her on anything for a few days. I laughed and told her it was because she had not given me a reason to do so. I also thanked her for reminding me to be as forthcoming with praise and affirmation as I was with coaching for performance.

Marco Kelly

Collaborative Approach

There are times when you need to make the decision, and there are times when the decision needs to be made through consensus. It is always imperative that your team knows which approach you are using in making the decision. If they believe it is a collaborative decision, but you will be making the final decision only looking to them for input and feedback, if your decision ends up being against what the team thinks, they will take it quite hard. In a situation like that, it is not only essential to communicate the type of decision being made, Collaborative or Sole, but also what the big picture reasons are for not going along with the consensus.

There are times, however, when a collaborative decision is best. There is the idea that people are more likely to go along with something they have helped create than something that has been communicated down to them. In my experience, I have found this to be true.

I had used this approach when it was pretty obvious what the right decision was, but the process of inclusion was necessary for the execution. Also, when the decision itself was crucial, and it was essential to get as many heads in the game as possible. We need to think of all the factors and possible outcomes to help choose the right path.

I have primarily used this approach for problem-solving. When faced with having to come up with a solution for a problem that the team members faced, who better to include in coming up with the solution than the team members themselves.

One Saturday morning, during a General Staff Meeting, a member

How To Build The Team You Want

of my team voiced an issue regarding gratuities for large groups. In many cases, the groups were made up of young sports players on their way to or from some sports tournament. The kids would end up not leaving any tips for the Server, and in some cases, some players would leave without paying so in many cases the Server either made no money or had to kick in a few dollars to settle the bills. This was obviously a big and tricky issue. I had to be sensitive to the Server's need to make gratuities, but also to make sure that service to these large groups was not compromised. Due to the servers making nothing, or worse having to pay money out of their own pocket to settle the bills, they were not eager to serve those tables. The customers deserved the best treatment, so there was a need to solve this problem for both sides; the customers and the servers. I was hesitant about just putting an auto gratuity on large parties, as I felt that might not solve the problem for the customers. If the server knew they were getting a gratuity regardless of the service they gave, there wasn't much incentive to deliver excellent service. Yet, I had to trust my servers, whom I hired and trained. I had to believe that they would give the best service they could. I also had to remember that they provided excellent service to those tables even when they thought there was a good chance they would make nothing or less on the table.

In the end, I felt this was something that we should decide together, but I had to make sure they could see the big picture. It was important for the servers to understand the importance of all customers and that whether they were in a group or not, did not minimize their importance to our business. We cannot give poor service to people because they are in a group, because they will not always be in a group, some may choose whether to return to our restaurant based on the service received and if they did, bring with them their friends or family.

I helped them understand that their service can influence future visits and future tips, etc. In the end, we created a few systems to implement when dealing with large groups that felt positively affected all parties. Because we did this together and the decision was made using a Collaborative Approach, the matter was closed to everyone's satisfaction, and everyone followed the plan. One of the processes we also implemented was improving how payments for large tables were handled as that was where things seemed to fall or slip through the cracks.

Through the initial and subsequent meetings about it, we were able to resolve most of the issues. In the end, some people just leave without paying, and either the business or the server has to make up the difference to settle the bills.

Another opportunity you have for using this approach is when you have a team member who seems to be very resistant to change. This is usually the case because, for some reason, change brings about fear. A great way to combat this fear is to use the Collaborative Approach with that particular individual and have them be very instrumental in creating the change. For some reason, that they were involved in creating the change alleviated the fear. I say alleviated, not eliminated because although the process involved in the change is one thing, the reason for the change is another. You have to really sell them on why the change is necessary. Either by convincing them that the current process is not achieving the desired result and you need their help in making the changes needed or by assuring them that the new process would create many and significant benefits to the team overall, including him or her.

Remember, the goal is the change itself, not the credit for the change. If you run a company or department, you do not need the individual glories of successful changes or ideas; you will get the overall recognition for how well your team is doing on the whole. The more generous you are with allowing your team to be involved in the process, the more they take ownership. Moreover, the more they take ownership, the more they start to think about how to make the company better. The more people you have thinking about how to be the best, the more chance you have of being the best. This is a great culture to have in your organization.

A potential challenge if this is having too many people trying to be the hero and wanting to have their ideas implemented. Remind your Team Members to focus on the roles, positions and contributions within their scope. That focus is crucial to succeeding as a Team. There is nothing wrong with having everyone thinking like Generals, but it is not good if everyone is acting like Generals. We still need foot soldiers. However, if we have foot soldiers who buy into the big picture and who grasp the Vision, they will outperform any foot soldier that is just 'following orders.'

So, early on, you have to lay out the ground rules for how ideas are brought forward, how the decisions will be made on which ideas are implemented and how. Be careful with how you react to ideas, even the most idiotic ideas must still be appropriately handled; otherwise you risk eliminating the safety. If your team does not feel safe in bringing an idea forward, because of how you might react to their idea and how you might make them look and feel in front of their team-mates, the well of ideas will dry up very quickly. If this happens, your team will begin to lose any interest in being involved in helping to push your company to the highest of heights.

So, remove the barriers for your team to provide their ideas and feedback so you can learn from their perspective what changes may need to be implemented. Provide support for them to feel safe and confident to express their ideas and allow you and your team to benefit from the experience, expertise, job knowledge and creative ideas presented using the Collaborative Approach.

Educational Approach

Many companies regard training as primarily a 'first-two weeks' type of thing and then you are on your own. However, the reality is that Training is constant, on-going and consistent. The kind of training offered is based on a few factors. For this approach, we look at how we help people learn how to think differently, rather than just do differently.

We all learn to do things in ways that make sense to us. They may not make sense to everyone else, but they make sense to us. If you have a Team Member that does something a certain way, the only way to get them to do it differently is to help them think differently about it.

An example of this is when I took over a struggling restaurant and was training my Host staff to greet guests at the door properly. Their way of greeting was, in my opinion, too casual and forgettable and achieved nothing. A couple would walk in; my non-smiling hostess would stand behind the counter and say: "Hi, table for two?" The guest would say yes, and my hostess would say: "Certainly. Right this way, please." Then she would take them to a table, lay the menus on the table and walk away leaving the guests to seat themselves and get settled.

Not a great way to start the occasion of dining out, is it? It is not bad, and some might think it is good, but it certainly was not great. It was not memorable, and it did not create any positive emotional reactions.

Now, before I could get into setting up a new way of greeting, I had to first educate them on non-verbal communication, and about going the extra mile.

We have learned that communication is seven percent verbal, thirty-eight percent is tonality, pitch, and rhythm, and fifty-five percent is body language. Sometimes it is not what we say, but how we say it. Also, we can say something in which there is another message that is communicated by how we say it. For example, I would teach the servers when approaching a table to say: "Good evening, ladies and gentlemen. My name is Marco, and I will be taking care of your dining experience this evening. Can I get you something to drink to start, or would you like a moment to settle in?"

Now, in that line, I say, "taking care of your dining experience" instead of "I will be your Server." One of the things I accomplish by that is elevating my status with the table and establishing professionalism. I communicate that I am their Host, not their servant and by so doing I am now in a better position to lead them in their dining experience, rather than just take their orders. I can now offer suggestions, up-sell to nicer wines, etc. Another important element is saying "dining experience." I have now lifted the event from something grabbing a bite, to an occasion. I have seen physiological changes with my guests at a table by saying things like this. They might have been slightly slouching, and then I greet them, and they sit more upright in their chairs. It is compelling.

Another thing I communicate in that Server greeting is that my time is not a concern. I am there for them, not the other way around. How do I demonstrate that? By asking if they require something now, or if they need a minute to settle in. By giving them a choice, I eliminate the flinch of asking me if they could have a moment, by offering them one. And, if they do not want a minute, I am there to find out what they would like. This choice lets them know that I am on their timetable, not expecting them to be on mine.

This is how I educate the servers. With the Hostesses, it was not much different. When we greet guests, how we smile warmly, welcome openly and really take a moment to focus on them and connect with them can do amazing things to get the guests in a positive mental state in preparation for an amazing dining experience. We can accomplish this if we take the right approach. If we do not, the greeting can fall flat.

I remember walking into a national chain restaurant, and the way the hostess greeted us was by holding her hands out to her sides and gesturing with her head for us to speak. Undoubtedly the absolute opposite of what I was trying to teach my door staff.

It is not enough though to tell them what to do or even why. They have to buy it. What outcome does my way achieve, what result does their way achieve and which is better? What outcome do we want to accomplish with our guests? Which way produces that outcome? And so on, and so on. Then I have them do role-playing with each other to get comfortable with it until it feels natural.

If I do not make them see that there is another way that makes more sense than their way, they will revert to their own way when I am not watching them, and if they can see that my way makes more sense, they will make the change. People almost always do what makes the most sense to them, even if it does not make sense to anyone else.

By demonstrating your skills and expertise you establish your ability to educate, then you offer that training and advice in a manner that ensures their receptiveness to your coaching.

Using this approach and using it well is a great way to have your team members view you as a mentor. Moreover, I can tell you; there is nothing more validating or rewarding as being chosen as a mentor by members on your team. It is a great honor and not to be taken lightly.

Motivational Approach

Have you ever worked on a project for a long time? Maybe a home project such as a renovation, painting the house or landscaping?

When you begin, you are all excited about what you are doing, but after a while, it starts to feel like just work, and you lose the excitement.

When that happens, that is when you need a dose of Motivation. Sometimes we need to remind ourselves what we are doing, what it looked like before, what it will look like when we are done and the progress we have made towards that end goal. Also, sometimes we need someone to help remind us of those things because our own negative mental state prevents us from motivating ourselves.

To continue working on the project with the same intensity as in the beginning, you need something to get that excitement back: a refueling of positive energy that drives you forward to completion. It is not an accident that so many people begin something that they do not finish. It is not because they were not committed or that they still do not want it to be done; they have just lost the excitement and are looking instead for something else to get them excited.

Well, this can happen with our team members as well, especially when in the process of a big 'turn the ship around' or 'get off the ground' phase. If you start up or take over a company or department that has been poorly run for a while, you are usually faced with a pretty long process of direction or redirection. It takes a while to build up momentum in the right direction.

Let us use the old car stuck in the mud analogy we used earlier. It is always tougher to get the car moving from a stationary position, but once you get it running, kinetic energy takes over, and it gets easier to push, unless you have to go uphill, in which case gravity can be a pain in the neck. Another example is how a car has different gears, it needs strong force energy, in the beginning, to get the car from stationary to moving so you put it in first gear, but as you build momentum, you can change gears to change the force from strength to speed as less energy is required to turn the wheels.

The process is the same with your company. In a start-up, you are in first gear, much energy needs to be applied to get things moving, but as you build up some momentum, it gets easier, and then you focus on building intensity and speed. It can sometimes be a long term process, and your team can start to lose the excitement they felt in the beginning. It is your job to refuel them as needed. Do not wait until you see evidence of a loss of motivation, because if you see evidence of a loss of motivation, then there might also be a loss of momentum. Be proactive. Remind your team what it looked like before, what it will look like in the end and how far they have come.

Set benchmarks in the progress plan that you communicate to your team. Small goals within the grand goal that become barometers of progress and that you and your team can celebrate. This will help to keep your team motivated, excited and engaged in continuing to build momentum for your company.

Communicative Approach

Remember that the key to communication is that it is a two-way street. Just conveying information is not communication. That is broadcasting. One of the vital ingredients in effective communication is the feedback loop. The process of having a dialogue with your team is crucial to ensure that the messages you are conveying are being received as they are intended.

The point of communicating is to be understood. If how you are saying things does not allow you to be understood, it is your job to find new ways of stating the message you are trying to communicate.

I remember many years ago speaking to a friend of mine who was trying to explain something to me. I was not getting what she was trying to say at all, and rather than find a different way to explain it, she just kept repeating over and over exactly what she had initially said, although she did seem to get a bit louder. When I told her flat out that I did not understand what she was trying to say, she said: "Well, I know what I mean."

I thought this was a funny thing to say. "Well, I know what I mean." This would be great if she were talking to herself, but the point of communication is to have the other person know what you mean.

When discovering that the person you are talking with does not understand you, find other ways of saying what you want to say. Do not just keep repeating the same thing over and over again. More volume does not produce clarity. Seek to be understood. Ask follow up questions to make sure that what you are trying to get across is actually coming across.

If you were trying to open a door with a key, but it was the wrong key, would you keep trying to open the door with the same key? Would try doing it louder to see if that works? Or would you try a different key?

One of the things I like to do, which may be evident to you by now from reading this book, is to tell stories. I find stories and analogies are great for building context into the message. Like the story I just told about the conversation I had with a friend of mine many years ago. Telling that story helped communicate the importance of understanding that it does not matter that you understand what you are trying to say, but that it is essential that your counterpart understands what you are trying to say. A great way to use the story or analogy tool is to find out what interests the person you are talking to and use their interests in your analogy so they can more easily connect to your message.

I do this a lot during leadership coaching. It helps to put things into perspective to my mentee to use things they like or know a lot about to illustrate my points. If they are into sports, I will use sports analogies. It is not hard to see that if I am talking to someone who has no interest in sports but is very much into the music scene that using sports analogies would not help me get my message across. Tailor the way you speak to whom you are talking.

There is an old saying that goes: Treat others the way you would like to be treated, but there is a flaw to this line of thinking; Personality types. Not only do different personality types communicate differently ranging from open and direct to closed and indirect, but different people like to be treated in different ways. Consider a sadist and a masochist; they do not want to be treated the same. Now I know that is a silly example, but you get the point.

If not, let me find another way of getting my message across.

Consider a high rolling stockbroker from Wall Street and a local potato farmer from Prince Edward Island. Would you talk to them the same way? Now, I certainly do not mean to imply that one is better than the other, just that their style of communicating and choice of words and phrases would be very different.

Here is another: Your little brother or sister, and your boss. Would you speak to them the same way? Now, unless your brother or sister was your boss, chances are you would talk more familiarly with your sibling than you would your boss.

The reality is that for the most part we instinctively adjust our speech style based on our perception of the person to whom we are talking. The challenge when it comes to your team members is that you might paint all or most of them with the same brush. Moreover, although their differences may not be as extreme as some of the examples I have listed, they do have differences. It would be best if you learned to pick up on those differences and adjust your style of speech in much the same way to be effective in communicating with your team members on their level.

Do not treat people the way you want to be treated, treat people the way they want to be treated.

Remember to ask follow up questions and seek confirmation from them that you are on the same page.

Another great tool of communication is Questions. Asking the right questions and properly can have a huge impact.

Here is an example of a question: How can I get fit?

Here is a better way to ask the question: How can I achieve and maintain a high fitness level?

Here is an even better way to ask the question: How can I achieve and maintain a high fitness level and have fun doing it?

Do you see where I am going?

Sometimes by digging a little deeper with your questioning, you can influence new lines of thinking with your team that can produce dramatic results. Sometimes you can lead a Team Member to a new way of looking at something just by asking the right question.

Evaluative Approach

To take an intelligent approach to effectively setting goals for your team members, it is imperative that you evaluate your team members on a predetermined set of attributes. A portion of this approach has been outlined in the Evaluation Process where you measure your team members against a pre-set of character and performance attributes to determine how to coach your Team Member for growth and development. In addition to this measure, another factor in evaluating your team member is their results.

Pam worked for me as a Marketing Coordinator for a restaurant. Pam had the most of the right attributes for character, and she had most of the right attributes for performance. Where she lacked at one point was in understanding that time and effort did not mean much if you were not producing results. At one point, during gentle coaching, she became a little defensive and stated that she was working her ass off and putting in many hours. To which I explained that I would prefer she worked half the time and half the effort and produced more. I showed her how she could work smarter and accomplish more by making good choices regarding her daily activities and where she focused the majority of her attention. We are all familiar with the Pareto principle, or the eighty-twenty rule, which states that we produce eighty percent of our results from twenty percent of our activities and twenty percent of our results from the other eighty percent of our activities. If we focus our attention on doing the activities that produce the lesser of our results, you would be working hard and putting in much time, with little effect. If you focused all your attention on doing those twenty percent of activities that produce eighty percent of your results, you would work easier and in less time and have higher productivity. The key is in identifying which of the activities are the eighty percent results activities and which are the twenty percent result activities. Do that, and then focus your time and attention on the highly productive activities and you will see great results.

Pam's problem was not that she failed to determine which activities were which. Her problem was that the low producing activities were her favorite activities and she was not drawn to performing the high producing activities. She procrastinated on the activities she did not want to do and spent as much time as she could on the activities she liked doing. Also, despite how much fun she was having, she could convince herself that she was working hard and putting in long hours.

I, however, was more concerned with results and less with the number of hours she was clocking. I was paying her a salary, not for hours, but results. I would not have cared if she worked ten hours a week but dramatically increased sales. Moreover, I did not care how many hours she worked if there was no increase in sales.

In using the Evaluative Approach, I again explained to her the objectives of the position. The objectives! This was the key. I explained that it was not important what she did with her time, or how much time she did it in, but only whether she was achieving the objectives of the position.

I evaluated the numbers with her, where we were, where we needed to be, what initiatives we needed to implement to drive us towards the reaching of those numbers and the activities we needed to focus on to achieve the results we wanted and needed to achieve. I helped her understand what needed to be done, what she needed to be doing. I also helped her realize that if there were things that she needed to do that she did not want to do, that she did not have to do them. She did not have to do any of it. I could find someone else to do them. I explained that certain activities required a specific personality type to be successful and if she felt

How To Build The Team You Want

she was not capable of being successful in the role because of her inability to perform those activities, that perhaps a different position or company or industry might be better for her.

The thing is I did not say any of that to manipulate her. I sincerely meant it. I do not want anyone to do something they do not want to do. However, if it needs to be done, then someone has to do it, and if they do not want to do it, then I'm sure I can find someone else who does want to do it.

Use the Evaluative Approach to highlight the third party references that have been established and communicated beforehand during the orientation process. Evaluate people based on a predetermined set of requirements and results for each position and determine whether their actions and performance are generating success for them in their job or not by comparing their actual results to the desired results. Identify with them the variances and set goals for them to close the gaps. This clear and concise approach is the key to being impartial when you need to approach your team members about performance.

Now to be effective with the Evaluative Approach you need to set aside some time to observe your team members in action.

You cannot effectively use the Evaluative Approach if you have no idea how your team members are performing, how they are carrying out their tasks, how they are interacting with each other, the customers, the management, etc.

You have to watch them and make notes. An important note here is not to go into the observational method with any agenda at all. Do not go in thinking that you are looking to catch people do things right, and do not go into it looking to catch people doing wrong. Have no predetermined conclusions about anything going in. The reason for this is that you will always find what you are looking for. Moreover, if you are focused on finding something you are looking for, it is very easy to miss seeing things that might amaze you, negatively or positively, because you went into it with a closed mind.

An example of this is the game of looking around the room and take notice of everything you see that is red. Take your time, when you feel you have noticed everything in the room that is red, close your eyes. Now think of everything in the room that is blue.

Because you were looking for the things that were red, you did not notice any of the things that are blue.

So when you are ready to begin observing your team, walk in stupid. 'Walking in stupid' is the idea of clearing your mind, and then opening your eyes to your surroundings as if you are seeing them for the first time.

I had a Bartender once whom I used to have to go to very frequently to tell him to tidy up the image of his bar. I referred to it as his bar, because I wanted to inspire a sense of ownership. It was not that he was dirty or messy; he just did not keep things neat. The bottles on the back of the bar were jumbled and not in any order, and he would leave things in places they did not belong. I had to go over and repeat this to him again and again, and he was not quite getting what I meant.

I remembered the old rule: If you have a problem, and you have tried everything, and the problem still exists, then the problem is you.

So I knew I had to find a new way to get him to see what I meant.

I was sitting at a booth across from the bar, and I called him over and asked him to sit with me. When he sat down, I asked him to look around the room at the tables, the windows, the chairs, the pictures on the wall, etc. Then I asked him to look at his bar and to tell me what he thought. He looked for a while, and a smile started to spread on his face. I asked him what was funny. He said, "I get it now." I asked, "Get what?"

He did not answer, but got up and went to tidy up the bar. When he was done, he came back out front and looked at it again. He looked over his bar, nodded and went back to work. We never had to talk about it again. All he needed was to see his bar the way his customers see his bar. He was so used to seeing the bar the way he always saw the bar that he stopped noticing when things were not right. I encouraged him to look at it with fresh eyes. I renewed his perception by having him look around the room from a different point of view. The tables and chairs were neat, the windows were dressed neatly, the pictures hung on the wall neatly, by comparison, his untidy bar stuck out like a sore thumb. He got it, and he fixed it.

When doing your observations, notice how people do the things they do, notice what they do not do, but just see it all for the first time each time. Do not try to find the answers you want to fit the questions you have; just look at it with fresh eyes and make a note of all the colors you see.

One of the systems I used to use was to write down the names of all of the team members on little slips of paper and put them in a cup, and then every day I would pull out one or two. If they were not coming in to work that day, I would pull out another name and put their name back into the cup. The goal was to empty the cup by the end of the month. By doing this, I had spent a portion of every day observing my team members individually and allowed myself the opportunity to see them as if I was seeing them for the first time. I would make notes about what I saw and then later I would evaluate them based on the criteria listed above. While observing one Team Member, I was not blind to the others, but I was more focused on the one whose name I had drawn from the cup. They had the bulk of my attention, but I still had to see everything else that was going on.

With this system and approach, when I would sit down with them and review them based on the Evaluation Criteria of Character and Performance attributes, I could cite actual events that supported the conclusions of my evaluation of them. By starting

Marco Kelly

with the facts, drawing the conclusions and approaching it in a helpful, supportive manner, it was a very empowering and motivational approach.

Accountability Approach

It is essential to have your team members understand the systems they work within. It is vital for them to understand that their actions, or lack thereof, produce certain consequences. If they fully understand this, then when some form of discipline needs to be executed, they are aware that it is their actions that have led to this discipline and not because you happen to be in a bad mood today or some other arbitrary reason.

I have found it necessary to ensure there is an abundance of clarity when it comes to expectations, policies, procedures, processes, methods, rules and regulations. It takes a lot of work and commitment to ensure there is clarity when it comes to these things, and if there are times when any of these can be waived or abandoned and who is allowed to approve of doing so.

This clarity is fundamental for the Accountability Approach as you cannot successfully hold your team members accountable when they are not aware of what they are being held accountable. Also, if there is any ambiguity regarding any of the elements listed, it will only serve to ensure that there is no standard in place at all for that element.

At one restaurant, I had spent a lot of time and effort in ensuring the team understood my expectations as they pertained to service standards. Thursday nights had typically been quiet, so we implemented some entertainment ideas to drive business up on that night. And it worked.

Typically I would only have two servers working in the Lounge, and they did quite well. However, as business began to pick up, I noticed that the service levels began to slide.

I approached the two servers and mentioned that I was thinking of bringing another server on for Thursday nights. Their reaction was exactly as I expected. "Please don't; we are finally making good money on Thursdays."

I mentioned that I had noticed the declining service levels and helped them recall my feelings about service and the steps we need to take every shift, every day to accomplish our goals, our Vision.

Then I said: "I tell you what, you prove to me that I do not have to bring another person on, and I will not." I will tell you something, I never had to bring another Server on to handle the business on Thursday nights, and we only got busier. They worked so well together and looked after everyone so well I am sure they lined their pockets quite well those nights.

So here is the deal: If I had gone up to them and told them that I needed them to work harder and make sure that the service standards were maintained, I would have received all kinds of excuses and resistance. However, by using the Accountability Approach, I put it to them to hold themselves accountable for the service standards and that if I were to bring another Server in on Thursday nights, it would be strictly due to their level of performance. They accepted that accountability because it would mean more money in their pockets. I gave them an opportunity to prove to me that they could do something amazing, and they did. Now, do not get me wrong, as much as I was prepared to bring an extra Server on to handle the business volume, I could never compromise service standards to save labor costs, I was glad I did not have to. I could save labor and ensure our service levels were maintained and our customers received the great experience we had promised them.

Another aspect of the Accountability Approach is in when you have to dismiss someone. If you have effectively used the Accountability Approach all the way through, when you have to dismiss someone, you simply lean on the expectations you have set,

How To Build The Team You Want

the standards, the policies, the rules, regulations, and so on, and compare the expectations to what was actually delivered by the employee, and even they can see that the reason for their dismissal is not personal, but founded on a history of low performance on their part when comparing their actual performance to the expected performance. Now, is this always going to be the case? No. The reason? People are not always rational and reasonable, especially when it comes to being fired. However, if you handle it the right way, it does not have to be messy.

I will tell you two stories about this:

I had to dismiss one of my Assistant Kitchen Managers once. I had my AGM (Assistant General Manager) sit in on the meeting with me. When I was done and the young lady left, my AGM looked at me and asked, "How in the world did you do that?"

Do what? Fire someone and have them smiling, shaking my hand and thanking me. How? I did not make it personal; I made it about the big picture. The type of person we needed in the position, the level of performance we needed from that person. I suggested that they were not happy because either the job or the company was not a natural fit for them. I told them that if I were to delay another day in dismissing her that I would be robbing a day from her life, a day that she could use to go and find the right position or company. I told her that I valued her as a person and saw that she had incredible potential to succeed at whatever she wanted to achieve, but that it was clear by her attitude and actions that she did not want to succeed in that position and that company. She knew that she could not dispute anything I said. She knew that if she were in my position she would be doing the same thing. She got it. She left. She found another job with another company, and I sincerely hope she found happiness there.

In another situation, I had another server who worked the late night shift in the dining room. I received a complaint on the phone from a guest who said they waited five minutes at the door around ten thirty in the evening. They began to think that the dining room side was closed and only the Lounge side was open. Finally, they saw a Server and asked if they could sit in the dining room. She said, "Sure." And the guests went and sat down. On the phone, the customer went on to tell me that they sat there without menus for another five minutes before the Server came over to them. By this time, they were upset, and the service did not get much better.

Now, we all know that things can get exaggerated when telling stories like these, so I had to be sure. Conveniently, we had cameras all over the restaurant, and I could review the footage from the night before to determine the validity of the complaint. They did exaggerate, but only slightly. It was three and a half minutes at the door and another three minutes at the table. Still, it was way too long and much longer than the times I had specified when I had trained my staff. The kicker, there was no one else in the restaurant. What was the Server doing when the guests sat themselves? She stood at the counter by the door and stared out the window.

In our meeting later that day after the phone call, I asked the Server if I had ever been ambiguous about how we look after our guests. She said no. I asked her if I had always been very clear and concise about how we greet guests and the level of service we provide. She said yes. I asked her if she only had one table, what level of service they should receive. She said the very best. I then proceeded to relay the information I had received from the guest and that the cameras had verified it. I explained to her that as she knew what was expected, and she knew how our guests were to be taken care of, there was no excuse for her actions. I told her that I now could not trust her to look after our guests and that if I could not trust her, she was done.

What could she do but accept that decision? She asked me not to let her go, but her actions demonstrated a complete lack of commitment to the goals and objectives of the company despite being very aware of what they were. I had worked with her in the past during training to help her understand the big picture. I had always worked to provide a happy, safe work environment for all my staff and opportunities to do their best. Her actions told the story that she did not care.

Moreover, I did not need people who did not care. I have always said to my team; there is nothing in this restaurant that you have to do if there are tasks or duties assigned to you that you do not want to do, that is ok. You do not have to do them. I am sure I can find someone who wants to do them, and they can have your job.

Accountability: it is on them.

Marco Kelly

Mirror Approach

You know those times when you are speaking to someone and what they are saying in words is very contrary to what they are saying with their tone, pitch, breathing pattern, and body language? Like those times when you are speaking with your spouse, and you can see that something is bothering them, but when you ask what is wrong they answer "Nothing!" Riiight....

When this happens, it is easy to see that something is wrong, but they say "nothing" usually because they are not ready or able to communicate what is going on, or they do not want to get into it at all. Well, we all know how to read the cues when someone's words are betrayed by all the other non-verbal cues and can tell when people are not honest. For example, you may have a team member who says they are committed to the Vision, but you can see from their actions and attitude that they are not. The Mirror Approach is how you relate to that Team Member the things that they are communicating non-verbally. I.e., Through their tone, pitch, body language or actions, and how those elements betray their real feelings despite how their words tell a different story.

I once had a girl working for me at a restaurant and despite all her efforts to hide her feelings; I could sense that something was wrong. I asked her about it, and she said that there was nothing wrong. I used the Mirror Approach and 'showed' her what I was seeing. I encouraged her to tell me what was wrong and did all I could to make her feel safe to express herself freely. She eventually went on to say to me that she was unhappy about the new schedule and thought that she was being punished for something because of the shifts she received. Wow!

Imagine how those feelings would fester had I not opened the dialogue and allowed the opportunity to help her understand the actual reasons behind the schedule.

The ensuing dialogue helped me to understand what her true desires were from a scheduling standpoint, and helped her understand my reasons for scheduling her in the manner that I did. It was not because I was punishing her, but it was because of how highly I thought of her and her ability to deliver fantastic service during crucial times.

It was also helpful for me to understand which shifts she preferred despite her previously telling me that she did not care which shifts she got so long as she was able to work about forty hours per week. This was another one of those opportunities where someone on your team may tell you something and not be completely open and honest about it.

From that point on, she felt a lot safer being open with me and it made for a much better relationship. I was able to factor her preferences into scheduling, and she was able to understand that when I scheduled her outside of those preferences, it was because I needed her and not because I was punishing her. I also made it a point from that point on to show her where I scheduled her outside of her preferences and explained to her why I needed her at those times.

Through all of this, she felt a lot better about working those types of shifts, and after a while, she told me that she quite enjoyed them now and that I could schedule her on those shifts more often. This is something that would never have been achieved had I not mirrored with her and opened the door for better and more open communication.

Another typical example of this is when someone brings up a point about something that happened in the workplace. They might ramble on quite passionately about what happened, but then add that it does not bother them, or they do not really care about it.

It is important to note that your observance of these non-verbal cues is crucial to your understanding of what is going on in your organization. If you do not address the issues, and instead accept the verbal story as the truth of how people are feeling, you will be missing significant opportunities to help your team develop a better understanding of what is going on. Also, address crucial issues that if left unattended could severely damage the foundation of your culture and thereby impede the team's ability to achieve the Vision.

If someone brings something up, despite how they may say that it does not matter, accept the fact that they would not have brought it up at all if it honestly did not matter. Address it and look for solutions. In the approach with the Team Member, you might gently indicate that the fact that they brought it up and how they related the information is not consistent with the idea that it does not matter to them. You could then ask them to describe how they feel about it and do everything you can to make them feel safe to express themselves freely. The more you understand about the situation, the better equipped you would be in knowing what needs to be done. Also, the safer you make the Team Member feel in expressing themselves, the more likely it is that they will come to you with issues. Not only would this deepen the relationships between you and your Team, but the more you know about problems in your organization, the more you can do what needs to be done to keep everyone on track and working towards the Vision in a safe and happy environment. I have seen too many organizations falter because they were completely unaware of the problems the teams faced, or of the existing issues amongst team members, and these issues became cancer that ate away at the positivity, productivity, and overall culture.

Never, under any circumstances, speak ill towards a member of your team who brings an issue up with you. This will undoubtedly eliminate safety, and they would never bring an issue up with you ever again. Trust me; you do not want that to happen. Ever.

Interrogative Approach

Simply put, the Interrogative Approach to Leadership is employing the process of asking questions to either ensure that things are on the right track or to get them on the right track. I was always in the habit of asking my team to tell me what they were currently working on. There is very little more frustrating than being told to do something that you are already in the process of doing or about to do. It makes you feel micromanaged and degraded. Alternatively, asking someone on your team what they are doing allows them the opportunity to fill you in on what is going on and then, if needed, you can dig a little deeper if necessary to uncover any gaps. See the following dialogue as an example:

Leader: Hi, Joan. How are things going?

Joan: Really good.

Leader: What are you working on right now?

Joan: Right now I am following up with the suppliers as their shipment today had some errors, and I am working with them to get it resolved.

Leader: Great. What else do you have on the go?

Joan: Negotiating with ABC for the new supply contract, finalizing the reports for Month End for the Accountants and setting up for the departmental meeting for later this week to cover off the new policy changes.

Leader: Anything else?

Joan: I think that is it.

Leader: Excellent. It sounds as though you have everything under control. By the way, where are we with the new training schedule for the new hires coming in next week?

Joan: Oh, sorry. Completely forgot about that. Will have that done and ready for your review by the end of the day.

Leader: Perfect. Thanks, Joan.

What this approach is designed to do is allow your team member to showcase what is going on and the follow up of "Anything else?" is intended to ensure that the item or items you are waiting for are on their radar, rather than you going to them and telling them what they have to do.

Another example of the Interrogation Approach is to keep asking questions to qualify the Team Member's comment or excuses. Here is an example from a conversation I had with a Kitchen Manager. Just so you understand the tone of the conversation, I was asking the questions in a somewhat playful manner with a smile on my face. I needed him to realize his own excuses weren't working without making him feel defensive.

Me: Chef, is there a reason for not having any Penne for a while during dinner service tonight?

Chef: We were busy.

Me: So you are saying that when we are busy, we can't perform well?

Chef: No, Boss. I asked the cooks to do it, but they said they would do it later.

Me: Oh, I see, so the cooks are running the kitchen now?

Chef: No, but we were busy.

Me: Ok, so let me see if I have this correctly: You only run the kitchen when we are not busy?

Chef: No…

Me: So what could we have done?

Chef: (Realizing he had no excuses) I should have been aware of it beforehand and directed my cooks to fix it. We could have thrown a pot of water on and cooked some off during service, Boss. It will not happen again.

Me: Thank you, Chef.

The idea behind this line was that no matter what my Chef said, I would qualify it to determine the validity of the statement. The point I wanted to make was that he was accountable for his kitchen, he should have either made sure we were adequately prepped, or if the business volume was higher than usual that we were monitoring our usage and watching inventory levels to make sure we were staying ahead of the game.

If I had approached it by addressing what should have been done, I would have encountered excuses. However, by using the Interrogation Approach and eliminating the excuses beforehand, all Chef had left was accountability for what happened and a commitment to how it would be handled in the future. My Chef in the above scenario was very good at making excuses, but he was also very good at accepting accountability when he had no excuses. So I knew I had to get the excuses out of the way so he would go down the path of accountability.

Mediator Approach

I was sitting in my office writing up a schedule for the following week when one of my team members, Dawn, came to me to tell me that another Team Member, David, was rude to her. What I could have done at that moment was to inquire with Dawn what David said or did that was rude and document and note everything that she says and then call David into my office and have a one-on-one chat with him about what Dawn said.

I have done this in the past, in my early days in management, and I learned a valuable lesson when it comes to these kinds of situations: People can sometimes lie.

On another occasion, I had a Chef come up to me to tell me that my Assistant General Manager had come into the kitchen to tell him about something, and had done so rudely and disrespectfully. My Chef was saying that my AGM was swearing and being belligerent. The thing was, I knew my AGM very well and knew that it was not in his nature to speak to people like that. So, I said to my Chef, "Derek would never swear."

My Chef looked at me and realized that he was not going to get away with lying and he agreed that Derek really did not speak that way. He did go on to say that he was upset that Derek came to him to tell him how to do his job. I could have asked my Chef at that moment if Derek was telling him how to do his job, or merely relaying feedback regarding an event so that he could know that a problem existed and could take steps to fix it, but I chose not to.

The best thing to do in these types of situations is getting as far away as possible from the He Said/She Said. So in both situations, I called them to meet with me together to relay what happened.

I have seen people become enemies over a misunderstanding that would have been cleared up in two minutes if someone had just asked: "Why did you do or say that? That really upset me," allowing the other person to clarify their intention and clear up any misunderstandings. One of the things I have learned is that people can jump to the wrong conclusion. Moreover, as I have said before, we do not react to the things that happen in life, but to our perception of what happened.

This typically happens when we are driving and someone cuts us off. The reflex reaction is to assume that the other driver is acting like he owns the road. We do not naturally give the benefit of the doubt. What if that other driver is in an emergency and is on the way to the hospital, or home due to an accident involving one of his children? Alternatively, what if they are just late for a very important appointment? Maybe it is their fault they are late, perhaps it was due to circumstances out of their control. However, the truth is that we do not think about any of it. We just usually jump to the conclusion that they are not a nice person. This is due to how we perceive the situation and to the stories we start to tell ourselves about what happened.

However, what if someone could come along and give you and the other person the opportunity to understand each other and to help you see things in a different light? That might allow you to tell different stories that would create a completely different perspective on the situation and that would then allow you to continue along without the negative emotions and stress of what you thought had happened?

Sounds like a big job. It is. And it is yours. Use the mediator approach to help your team members understand each other during a conflict and clear up any misunderstandings. Is it always going to work? No. Why? Cause sometimes that other driver really is just an A-hole.

Catalyst Approach

Every team needs a Catalyst, someone within the organization that helps to drive everyone in the right direction. Some Managers make the mistake of promoting their best team members to supervisors or managers. Sometimes those team members do not want promotion as they are happy working the day to day functions of their job. I saw this happen a lot, especially in the Restaurant Industry. A Server or Bartender who was really good and did their job well was promoted to Manager or Supervisor. They did not really want the 'promotion' as it usually meant more hours, more work, more responsibility and less money. And, in many cases, the fact that they were good at their jobs did not mean they were going to be good leaders.

If you have members who are really good, before promoting them, find out if that is the direction they want to go. If it is, begin a grooming process to prepare them for that role when they get there. If not, then help them become Catalysts for the rest of the team.

This makes the process of getting everyone pushing in the same direction much easier as someone from within the team is 'rallying the troops' as it were and helping to get things on track more effectively.

A Catalyst can do things within the team that the head leader cannot. A Catalyst can find out about things within the team that would often get hidden from the Leader. If you can get a Catalyst in your team, this will help. You do not need them coming and reporting everything to you, but the reality is that you do need them to help you 'Navigate the Norms' within the team and push for higher productivity, more positivity, more accountability, etc.

The more Catalysts you have, the better.

Consider you have a team of ten. With no Catalysts, or Internal Champions, it is one against ten. If you can recruit a Catalyst, it is now two against nine. One more would be three against eight. You get the picture.

The more Catalysts you have on your team, the less resistance you will have to change and the higher percentage of the team taking an ownership attitude in driving the function of the team.

You could almost make being a Catalyst in the team seem very desirable as in, being a part of your Inner Circle. If done well, others will aspire to be there as well. It depends on the overall sense of your team and your relationship with them.

An example would be if you have a team that is not one hundred percent with you. Perhaps you have just inherited the team, and you have not entirely won them over yet. You can still look for Catalysts, but you might not want to make it evident that they are a part of your Inner Circle as that may only serve to alienate them from the rest of the group.

The Catalyst, however, in that situation, could slowly help you by opening the rest of the team's mind about you.

To identify the right candidate for Catalyst, look for someone confident and secure. Someone the rest of the team seems to respect and admire. Someone who almost seems to march to the beat of their own drum and is not worried too much about what other people think someone who appears to have an inherent sense of pride in his or her work and who holds himself or herself to a higher standard.

If you have someone like that on your team, begin grooming them for the Catalyst role. All you really have to do is spend some extra one-on-one time with him or her and help them understand more clearly the big picture of the goals, objectives and plan for

How To Build The Team You Want

the company (otherwise known as the Vision). The more they know that, and the more they understand how they can help influence others to contribute to the Vision, if they are the right candidate, they will take it upon themselves to be that Catalyst that your team needs. If you make it official with the candidate, you could also include some incentive rewards based on measurable goals for Team performance.

This way that individual does not have to compromise their pay and lifestyle can continue doing the things they love to do, and yet feel as if they are playing a more significant role in the success of the organization and the team. If done right, the Catalyst Approach can be a very powerful way to drive your team to High Performance.

In some cases, choosing someone who has the skills, but not the right attitude to be a Catalyst can have a huge and dramatic and positive effect on their attitude. They would direct their focus to be the best they can be to set an example for the rest of the team. I have seen it with my own eyes. It was a fantastic thing to experience.

Incentive Approach

One of the first things you would learn in sales is that the person you are trying to sell to always has the question in their mind: WIIFM ("What's in it for me?")

Whether we realize it or not, whenever anyone is trying to sell us something, a product, service or even an idea, this question is at the root of our thinking. There is very little, if anything, you do that does not serve you in some way. Do not be offended by that; it is just the reality of it. We are driven to help ourselves; some are just better at it than others.

Here is a scenario: You are walking down the street, and you see a man begging for money, you feel sorry for the man, so you put some money in his cup. Have you just sacrificed yourself for someone in need?

When you feel compassion for someone in a bad situation, it makes you feel bad. People do not like to feel bad, so when they do, their first instinct is to do something to take the bad feeling away, so by giving money, you take away the bad feeling and feel pretty good about yourself because you helped someone.

Now do not get me wrong. The beautiful thing in that scenario is that you actually felt compassion. You did feel bad. So many people these days walk by that begging man and feel nothing, and, by the same logic, because they feel nothing, they do nothing. Some even tell themselves that giving to the man would be a bad thing and twist the whole thing around so that they can feel good about themselves for not helping someone in need. That is how powerful WIIFM can be.

We are always on the lookout for how we can better our situation.

How To Build The Team You Want

Our beliefs and philosophies or our sense of ethics, integrity or morals is what keeps us from taking advantage of others and try to achieve better things for ourselves without it being at the expense of others. However, if push comes to shove, we are thinking of ourselves and our loved ones first.

When you understand the idea of WIIFM, you appreciate that with your team members there exists within the process of pushing themselves more to achieve some gain for the company the idea that there is some personal gain. That gain could exist in many different forms and formats: recognition, social acceptance, monetary reward, position enhancement, etc. Moreover, part of your job is learning the individual WIIFM for each member of your team, and what is the WIIFM for the team as a whole.

When I used to hold incentive contests to increase sales, I tried all sorts of things. If it were a dessert sales contest, the server who won would get to enjoy a dessert of their choice. I am sure you could already see the flaw in that; it only appeals to people who like dessert. What if I made it a beer or cocktail, then that would only appeal to people who drink. In the end, I made it a five dollar coupon that they could use for whatever they wanted. They could buy a drink, a dessert, save them up to take their spouse or even their family out for a meal, etc. This now appealed to everyone and soon everyone was engaged in the contest instead of only a few.

You might ask, well if it is their job to sell, why not just direct them to do their job. Cause you gotta make it fun sometimes. You gotta make it exciting. Create some fun rivalry, more focus, some re-engagement, etc.

Sometimes you dangle the carrot to develop a habit, or to prove they can do it if they put their minds to it, thereby setting a precedent. I once put an incentive in place for my entire kitchen team during a Friday night dinner, the busiest night of the week. The challenge was that if all the meals came out in good time, with no errors and no complaints from the customers, everyone on the team would be able to sit at the bar and enjoy two drinks on the house at the end of their shift. I knew my team and I knew getting a couple of drinks at the end of the shift was one thing, to do it together was another, and to be able to hang out in the bar together after work to do that was an essential item.

The first night we did this was not perfect, but they came close. I told them they could have one drink, but it would be brought back to the kitchen for them. The next week they pushed harder and it was perfect. Now here were my crossroads, do I maintain the incentive to get that level of performance, or do I use their performance on that night as a new benchmark for expectations. The key is, now they knew they could do it, so they could not use all the excuses they had before. The idea of an incentive approach is that it is perceived as an incentive. If I had done it all the time, it would become expected. It might then be regarded as a failing if they did not receive it rather than a reward when they did. So I only did it sometimes.

My expectations of performance was always the same, and now I was holding them to a high level of performance and presenting it that if they produced anything less was certainly a failing on their part (all of this done gently and playfully, of course). However, now and then, I would throw in the incentive to keep the fires burning.

Rewarding the whole team is fantastic. You can really create cohesion in a team when they are all working together to achieve something. I wanted to increase my customer average, so I incented my servers and bartenders to do so. I told them where we were currently, where we needed to be and that if we got there, we would have a staff party. Everyone was involved, even the Hostesses and the kitchen staff. I outlined all the different ways that guest average could be impacted, both negatively and positively. The goal was to get to the goal GA (Guest Average) and maintain it for a minimum of six weeks.

They got their party. We kicked in the food and got our beer and liquor suppliers to kick in for the drinks. They had a blast. The reality was that by maintaining it for six weeks, I was able to get the entire team to create new habits when it came to looking after guests that allowed them to continue to maintain and even elevate the GA. The bonus for them, it also helped them to make more tips. The other bonus, our guests were never happier. I was pleased, the team was happy, the customers were delighted, the shareholders were happy. Happiness all around. This all happened because I dangled a carrot for the whole team.

Now you can go and dangle carrots as well for the individuals on your team.

Going back to the Evaluations, when you set goals for more attributes, incorporate some incentive to get them even more engaged in adopting those deficient attributes and answering that question that you know will be in their minds: What is in it for me?

THE FINISH LINE

The goal of every Leader is to get the team to the finish line, to win the game of business and be successful, profitable, and happy and to have created or achieved something meaningful.

There is a price for success, and that price is sacrifice. Everyone on the team has to be willing to sacrifice for the team. Sacrificing time, energy, effort, emotion, blood, sweat and tears to make magic happen as a team.

There is something so profoundly beautiful about seeing a group of people come together with mutual purpose and pool their talents, energies, and efforts to accomplish amazing things.

If you have a team now or will have one someday, seek to bring them together under the umbrella of a higher purpose. It does not yield significant results when you trivialize the process of building a business or building a brand. Unless you are running a web business that does not require any other people, just you, then you can't do it without other people. Moreover, the chances are that if you are running that kind of business, you would not need to be reading this book.

You can't do it alone. You can't build your business on the backs of others unless they are emotionally and mentally invested in the Vision you have for your company. You can't build your brand on the backs of people who are only in it for a paycheck. The

How To Build The Team You Want

reason you can't do that is because if the people on your team do not care about your Vision, they will not be working to help you achieve it. Instead, they will be working to satisfy their own agenda despite how it may go against your Vision.

Can you imagine a football game? Two teams, all suited up and taking to the field. One team, however, does not want to be there. The Coach spent the last half hour in the locker room making them feel small, weak and resentful. The other team's coach just spent the last half hour building his team's confidence, filling them with fight and passion and the desire to conquer the world.

Would you say it is pretty easy to pick which team would win the game?

Every day you go to work and work with your team members, you have a choice to be one of those coaches. Which one do you think you should be?

The goal of this book was to give you some tools and philosophies to help you be the type of coach that sends your players on to the field filled with confidence, fight, passion and determination to bring home the trophy.

Create your Vision, make it meaningful, and then when you have successfully built your team; lead them to Victory!

About the author

Marco is a professional motivational speaker whose goal is to inspire people to utilize the 'Key Tools' to achieve the goals and objectives for all areas of their lives. With over 20 years of experience as a leader in the hospitality Industry and working as a coach and mentor for numerous people, Marco has developed a common sense approach to leadership by using analogies and stories to paint pictures of how things can be and how to make them happen.

Using an approach of Accountability and 'Connecting to the Vision', Marco has been able to generate success for companies he was hired to run, and in assisting other operators and owners, as a consultant, in generating growth and positive change in their companies.

Marco began working in the Hospitality Industry at the age of 14 and began his leadership career at the age of 21. Because of his inherent commitment to excellence his goal was to become the best leader he could be and so he became a dedicated student of Leadership, Coaching and Mentorship. Then, by taking principles and testing them out during his own experiences, Marco has been able to generate a list of the 'Key Tools', principles and philosophies that is the recipe for great leadership.

>   www.marcokelly.ca

www.ingramcontent.com/pod-product-compliance
Lightning Source LLC
Chambersburg PA
CBHW021823170526
45157CB00007B/2670